I0415758

Vegetation Classification and Mapping of Tallgrass Prairie National Preserve

Project Report

Natural Resource Report NRR/HTLN/NRR—2011/346

Kelly Kindscher[1]*
Hayley Kilroy[1]
Jennifer Delisle[1]
Quinn Long[1]
Hillary Loring[1]
Kevin Dobbs[2]
Jim Drake[3]

[1]Kansas Natural Heritage Inventory
Kansas Biological Survey
University of Kansas
2101 Constant Ave.
Lawrence, KS 66047

[2]Kansas Applied Remote Sensing Program
Kansas Biological Survey
University of Kansas
2101 Constant Ave.
Lawrence, KS 66047

[3]NatureServe
P.O. Box 9354
St. Paul, MN 55109

*contact kindscher@ku.edu

April 2011

U.S. Department of the Interior
National Park Service
Natural Resource Program Center
Fort Collins, Colorado

The National Park Service, Natural Resource Program Center publishes a range of reports that address natural resource topics of interest and applicability to a broad audience in the National Park Service and others in natural resource management, including scientists, conservation and environmental constituencies, and the public.

The Natural Resource Report Series is used to disseminate high-priority, current natural resource management information with managerial application. The series targets a general, diverse audience, and may contain NPS policy considerations or address sensitive issues of management applicability.

All manuscripts in the series receive the appropriate level of peer review to ensure that the information is scientifically credible, technically accurate, appropriately written for the intended audience, and designed and published in a professional manner.

This report received informal peer review by subject-matter experts who were not directly involved in the collection, analysis, or reporting of the data. Data in this report were collected and analyzed using methods based on established, peer-reviewed protocols and were analyzed and interpreted within the guidelines of the protocols.

Views, statements, findings, conclusions, recommendations, and data in this report do not necessarily reflect views and policies of the National Park Service, U.S. Department of the Interior. Mention of trade names or commercial products does not constitute endorsement or recommendation for use by the U.S. Government.

This report is available from http://web.ku.edu/~kindscher/tallgrass and the Natural Resource Publications Management website (http://www.nature.nps.gov/publications/nrpm/).
Please cite this publication as:

Kindscher, K., H. Kilroy, J. Delisle, Q. Long, H. Loring, K. Dobbs, and J. Drake. 2011. Vegetation mapping and classification of Tallgrass Prairie National Preserve: Project report. Natural Resource Report NRR/HTLN/NRR—2011/346. National Park Service, Fort Collins, Colorado.

NPS 031/107299, April 2011

Contents

Contents (continued)

Figures

Tables

Appendices

Executive Summary

The Tallgrass Prairie National Preserve (TAPR) encompasses 10,894 acres in eastern Kansas, just north of Strong City. This park unit was created on November 12, 1996 and is the first to protect a nationally significant example of the once vast tallgrass prairie ecosystem. Of the 400,000 square miles of tallgrass prairie that once covered the North American continent, less than four percent remains, primarily in the Flint Hills. The park unit is primarily rocky upland prairies and deep-soiled prairies in the lowlands. It also contains some wet prairie ravines, riparian forests and some former cropland and restored prairie.

A three-year program was initiated to complete the task of mapping and classifying the vegetation at TAPR. The Kansas Biological Survey (KBS) in conjunction with NatureServe developed a vegetation classification using the National Vegetation Classification System and produced a digital vegetation map. To classify the vegetation, plots located throughout TAPR were sampled during the summer of 2008. Additional data were obtained from vegetation plots sampled by the Inventory & Monitoring program in 2006. Analysis of the plot data by KBS produced 12 map units (eight vegetated and four land-use) which are directly matched to corresponding plant associations and land-use classes. Descriptions and a field key for all plant communities of TAPR are included in this report. Draft maps were printed, field tested, reviewed and revised. Accuracy assessment (AA) data points were collected on 112 data points in 2009 by KBS and used to verify the map's accuracy.

Introduction

Tallgrass Prairie National Preserve Vegetation Mapping Project

The Tallgrass Prairie National Preserve (TAPR) Vegetation Mapping Project was organized and coordinated by the Kansas Biological Survey (KBS) at the University of Kansas, in cooperation with NatureServe, in accordance with the standards set forth by the U.S. Geological Survey (USGS) – National Park Service (NPS) Vegetation Mapping Program.

The TAPR Vegetation Mapping Project was initiated because the preserve protects a nationally significant example of the once vast tallgrass prairie ecosystem. Of the 400,000 square miles of tallgrass prairie that once covered the North American continent, less than four percent remains, primarily in the Flint Hills. Although the Tallgrass Prairie National Preserve had been mapped at a coarse level (tallgrass prairie vs. riparian forest area), a more accurate map was needed to break out grassland types, rock outcrops, replanted vegetation, water, and other landmarks to National Vegetation Classification alliance. A unified objective classification, such as outlined in the National Park Service's Vegetative Mapping Program, can become a valuable aid to the preserve for the use in vegetation management, grazing, fire, and monitoring wetlands and wildlife. Since the National Park Service is charged with conserving, protecting, and interpreting the resources of this prairie landscape, an accurate and detailed vegetation map and data layers for a GIS is very useful for management purposes.

Common to all Vegetation Mapping Program projects, the three major components of the TAPR Vegetation Mapping Project are vegetation classification, vegetation mapping, and map accuracy assessment. In this report we discuss each of these fundamental components in detail.

USGS-NPS Vegetation Mapping Program

The National Vegetation Mapping Program is an interagency initiative established to inventory, classify, describe, and map vegetation in National Park units and other areas across the United States. It is administered by the USGS Center for Biological Informatics and the NPS Natural Resources Information Division, and provides baseline vegetation information to the NPS Inventory and Monitoring Program (I&M).

Vegetation Mapping Program scientists developed procedures for classification, mapping, and accuracy assessment (The Nature Conservancy [TNC] and Environmental Systems Research Institute [ESRI] 1994a).

Use of the National Vegetation Classification System (NVCS) as the standard vegetation classification system is central to fulfilling the goals of this national program. This system:

- is vegetation based;
- uses a systematic approach to classify a continuum;
- emphasizes natural and existing vegetation;
- uses a combined physiognomic-floristic hierarchy;
- identifies vegetation units based on both qualitative and quantitative data;
- is appropriate for mapping at multiple scales.

The use of the NVCS and the USGS-NPS vegetation mapping protocols facilitates effective resource stewardship by ensuring compatibility and widespread use of the information throughout the NPS as well as by other federal and state agencies. These vegetation maps and associated information support a wide variety of resource assessment, park management, and planning needs. In addition they can be used to provide a structure for framing and answering critical scientific questions about vegetation communities and their relationship to environmental conditions and ecological processes across the landscape.

The NVCS has primarily been developed and implemented by The Nature Conservancy (TNC) and the network of state natural heritage programs over the past twenty years (TNC and ESRI 1994a; Grossman et al. 1998). The NVCS is currently supported and endorsed by multiple federal agencies, the Federal Geographic Data Committee (FGDC), NatureServe, state heritage programs, and the Ecological Society of America. Refinements to the classification occur in the process of application, leading to ongoing proposed revisions that are reviewed both locally and nationally.

Vegetation Mapping Program Standards
The NPS I&M Program established guidance and standards for all vegetation mapping projects in a series of documents:

Protocols
- documenting a National Vegetation Classification System (TNC and ESRI 1994a);
- standards for field methods and mapping procedures (TNC and ESRI 1994b);
- producing rigorous and consistent accuracy assessment procedures (TNC et al. 1994);
- establishing standards for using existing vegetation data (TNC 1996);

Standards
- National Vegetation Classification Standard (FGDC 1997);
- Spatial Data Transfer Standard (FGDC 1998b);
- Content Standard for Digital Geospatial Metadata (FGDC 1998a);
- United States National Map Accuracy Standards (USGS 1999);
- Integrated Taxonomic Information System (http://www.itis.gov/);
- program-defined standards for map attribute accuracy and minimum mapping unit.

These documents are available on the USGS-NPS Vegetation Program Web site (http://biology.usgs.gov/npsveg/standards.html).

Tallgrass Prairie National Preserve
In November of 1996, federal legislation was passed creating the 10,894 acre Tallgrass Prairie National Preserve in the Flint Hills region of Kansas, located in Chase County, Kansas, outside of Strong City. Ownership of the park is a unique private/public partnership between the National Park Service and The Nature Conservancy. The preserve protects a nationally significant example of the once vast tallgrass prairie ecosystem.

Tallgrass Prairie National Preserve was created on November 12, 1996 to "...preserve, protect, and interpret for the public an example of a tallgrass prairie ecosystem..." and to "...preserve and interpret for the public the historic and cultural values represented on the Spring Hill Ranch."

The preserve is a designated National Historic Landmark that, "...outstandingly represents the transition from the open range to the enclosed holdings of the large cattle companies in the 1880's." In addition, the nomination notes that "...the ranch lands (contributing site) have retained a high

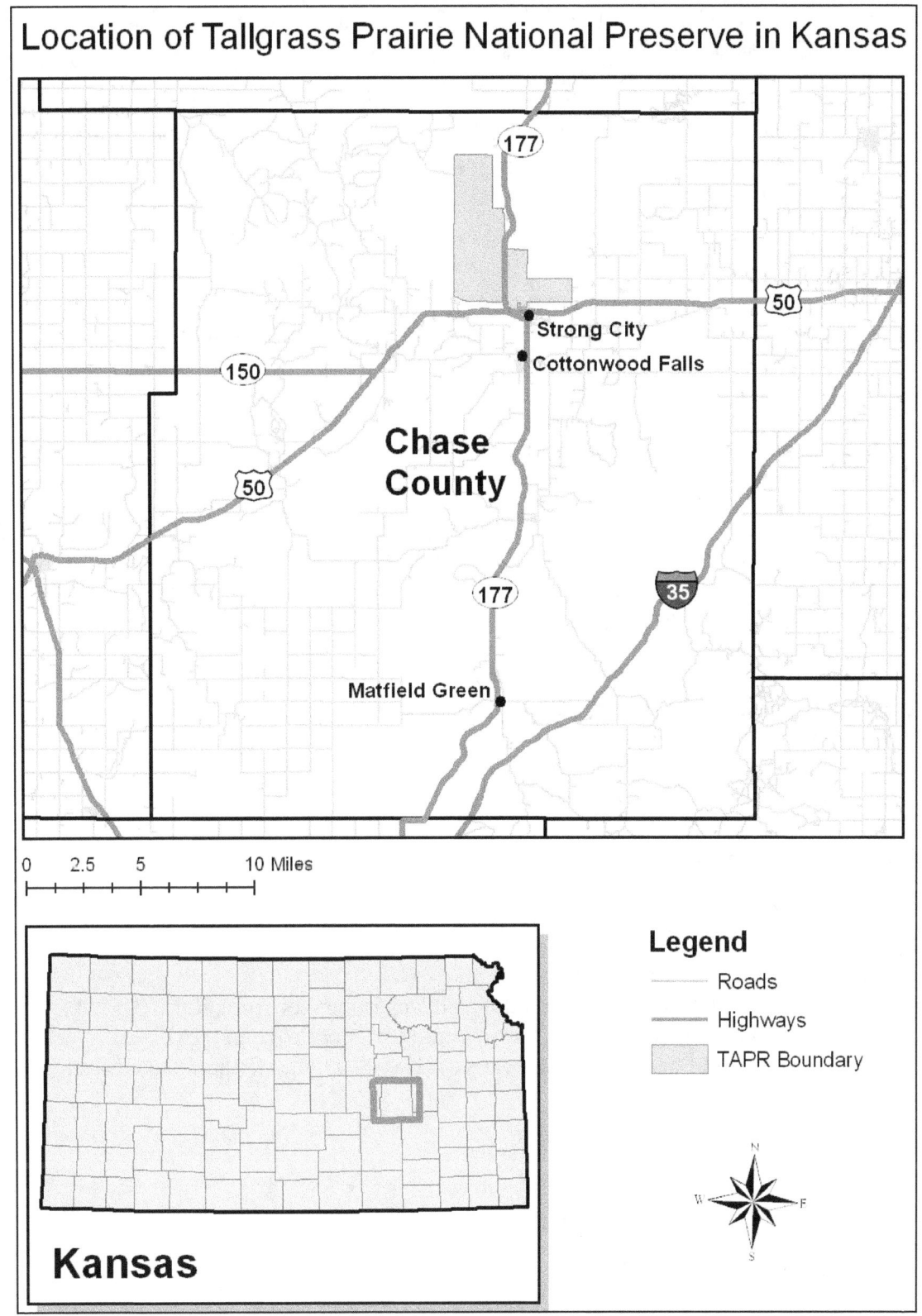

Figure 1. Location of Tallgrass Prairie National Preserve in Chase County, Kansas.

level of integrity in all areas of consideration: location, setting, feeling, design, materials, workmanship, as well as association" (Wolfenbarger and Nimz 1996)

The preserve was established to provide visitors access to the cultural and natural features of the Spring Hill/Z Bar Ranch. The preserve actively uses large grazers, i.e. bison and cattle, to manage the natural landscape and represent the cultural landscape.

Project Statistics

Field Work Summers of 2008 and 2009:
> Plot Sampling = 77 Plots:
>> 54 plots sampled in July 2008 by the Kansas Biological Survey staff
>> 23 plots sampled during the 2008 growing season by the Heartland Network

> Accuracy Assessment Points = 132
>> 112 points to assess vegetation classification
>> 20 additional points to assess presence of seeps
>> All collected in July 2009 by the Kansas Biological Survey staff

Classification:
>> 6 NVC Plant Associations
>> 2 Park Special Vegetation Classes
>> 4 Non-Vegetated Land-Use Classes

GIS Database 2006 – 2009:
> Project Size = 18,805 acres (7610.11 hectares)
>> Tallgrass Prairie National Preserve = 10,894 acres (4408.65 hectares)
>> Environs = 7,911 acres (3201.47 hectares)

> Base Imagery acquired from the NPS:
>> Fall 2005 IKONOS image

> Ancillary Imagery acquired by the Kansas Applied Remote Sensing Program, a program of the Kansas Biological Survey:
>> June and September of 2008 IKONOS image
>> 2003, 2004, 2005, 2006, and 2008 United Stated Department of Agriculture (USDA) Farm Service Agency National Agriculture Imagery Program (NAIP)
>> 2002 and 1991 United States Geological Survey (USGS) Digital Orthophoto Quarter Quads (DOQQs)
>> 1938 panchromatic imagery

> Minimum Mapping Unit = 0.5 hectare
> Total Size = 569 Polygons
> Average Polygon Size = 33.0 acres (13.35 hectares)
> Overall Thematic Accuracy = 92.0%
> Project Completion Date: 06/30/2010

Methods

The entire map extent is 18,730 acres, of which the park comprises 10,861 acres (Figure 2). The national standard minimum mapping unit is 0.5 ha, but some polygons, notably those of seeps or thin-soiled rocky areas, are smaller than the minimum mapping unit.

The vegetation mapping project at Tallgrass Prairie National Preserve was considered to be in the "medium park" category based on the overall size of the project area (TNC 1994b). As such, the standard methodology for sampling and mapping is to visit the entire park and select representative sites. It is assumed that these sites will sufficiently characterize the vegetation types and explain their distribution across the park without having to survey each stand of vegetation. Based on this approach the assignment of responsibilities was divided into five major tasks, including the following:

1. Plan, gather data, and coordinate tasks;

2. Survey TAPR to understand and sample the vegetation;

3. Classify the vegetation using the field data to NVC standard associations and alliances and crosswalk these to recognizable map units;

4. Acquire current digital imagery and interpret the vegetation from these using the classification scheme and a map unit crosswalk;

5. Assess the accuracy of the final map product.

All protocols for this project as outlined in the following sections can be found in documents produced by TNC and ESRI (1994a, 1994b) and TNC et al. (1994) for the USGS-NPS Vegetation Mapping Program. These documents can be found at: http://biology.usgs.gov/npsveg.

Planning, Data Gathering and Coordination

A scoping meeting was held in June 2007 with all project participants (Kansas Biological Survey, NatureServe, Tallgrass Prairie National Preserve staff, NPS Heartland Network staff, Homestead National Monument staff, National Park Service National Vegetation Mapping staff, and The Nature Conservancy). KBS was responsible for plot sampling and reconnaissance visits of potential community types of TAPR. KBS was also responsible for entering these data into a digital database, classifying these data, and providing a list and global descriptions for the TAPR plant associations. KBS was responsible for the imagery interpretation and creating a digital vegetation map and spatial database. NatureServe reviewed and evaluated the draft classification and wrote vegetation descriptions for all associations. KBS created a vegetation key, and conducted accuracy assessment of the vegetation map. NatureServe and TAPR staff provided logistical and technical support, and helped coordinate activities.

Field Survey

The field methods used by the Kansas Natural Heritage Inventory in sampling and classifying the vegetation followed the methodology outlined by the USGS-BRD/NPS Vegetation Mapping

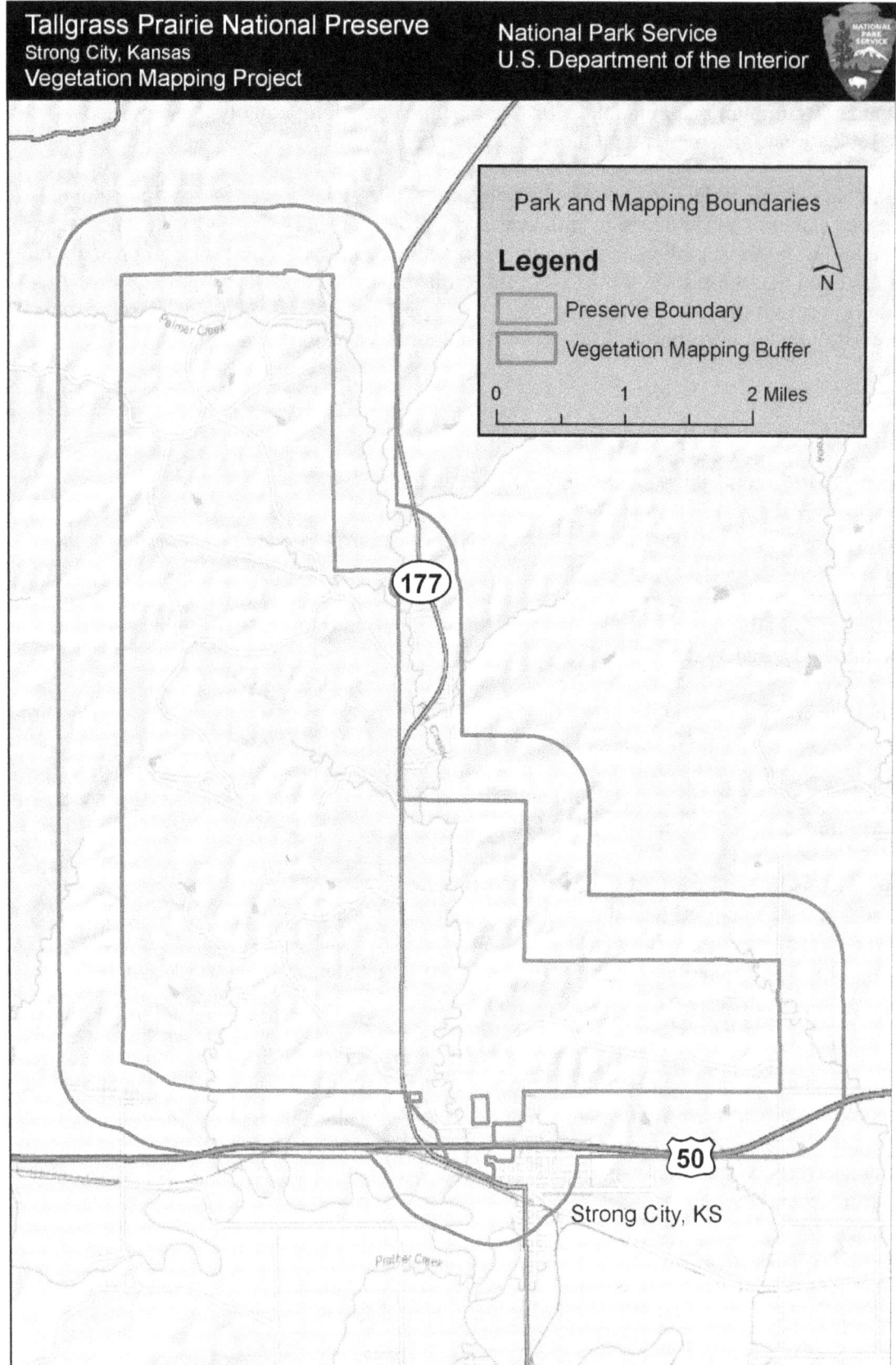

Figure 2. Map of the vegetation project boundary and park boundary.

Program and the NVC (Grossman et al. 1994, Grossman et al. 1998). The application of these methods to Tallgrass Prairie National Preserve is outlined below.

Vegetation data were collected in characteristic plots by KBS in July 2008 and from additional plot information acquired from the Heartland Inventory and Monitoring Network (Figure 3). Characteristic plots were located in areas that were visually representative of the preliminary vegetation categories. Plots were 100 m^2 in area, and GPS coordinates were recorded with a Garmin receiver. To maintain consistency with other projects in Kansas, plots were square. For a couple of the seeps in was actually necessary to make rectangular plots totaling 100m^2 in area due to irregular shapes of the feature. The accuracy for all of the recorded points ranged from 1-7 meters in horizontal accuracy, as recorded by the GPS receiver. Ten plots were sampled for most preliminary vegetation types: rocky mixed prairie, restored prairie, riparian vegetation, and brome fields. For "weedy" vegetation, only four characteristic plots were sampled due to the low abundance of the vegetation type. Ten plots were also sampled for springs and seeps, which were not characterized as a polygon vegetation type, but were mapped as points from Kansas Geological Survey data.

All plants found within the characteristic plots were identified to species level where possible. In a few cases, identification was only possible to the genus level (i.e., non-reproductive *Muhlenbergia* and *Carex* species). Visual estimates of percent cover were made for all species, including live material and the current year's standing dead. To maintain consistency with local vegetation surveys and other work of KBS, a continuous range of possible cover estimates was used, rather than cover classes. Plants found to cover at least one half of one percent of the plot were assigned one percent (0.01) and those with less than one half of one percent a "trace" (T). Also to maintain consistency with published accounts and similar projects in the region, species were assigned names following the Flora of the Great Plains (McGregor and Barkley 1986). An updated synonymy was completed when data were entered into the PLOTS database. Noteworthy surrounding vegetation, slopes, unusual soil features, and noticeable use by animals were also noted at each plot. Most plots were on a gentle slope with an A horizon of silty clay loam soils.

Additional plot data were obtained from the Heartland Inventory and Monitoring Network (James et al 2009). Tallgrass prairie sampling was conducted in 2008 on ten permanent plots. Each plot comprises two, 50 m long transects with ten sets of nested subplots systematically arranged. Working from the smallest to the largest plot, all herbaceous, woody shrub and tree seedling and sapling species were identified. Foliar cover was estimated in the 100 m^2 subplot using a modified Daubenmire (1959) scale. Forest overstory data were obtained from a breeding bird survey conducted in 2008, in which overstory trees were tallied in 18 plots (Peitz et al 2008).

Vegetation Classification

Upon completion of field surveys, all recorded data were entered into the NPS PLOTS database (TNC 1997), a Microsoft Access-derived program. The PLOTS database was developed specifically for the NPS vegetation and mapping program so that the electronic data entry fields mirror the standard field form. Data entry was facilitated by assigning each plant taxon a unique, standardized code and name based on the PLANTS database developed by Natural Resources Conservation Service in cooperation with the Biota of North America Program (USDA and NRCS 2009). Data was thoroughly proofed after entry to minimize errors.

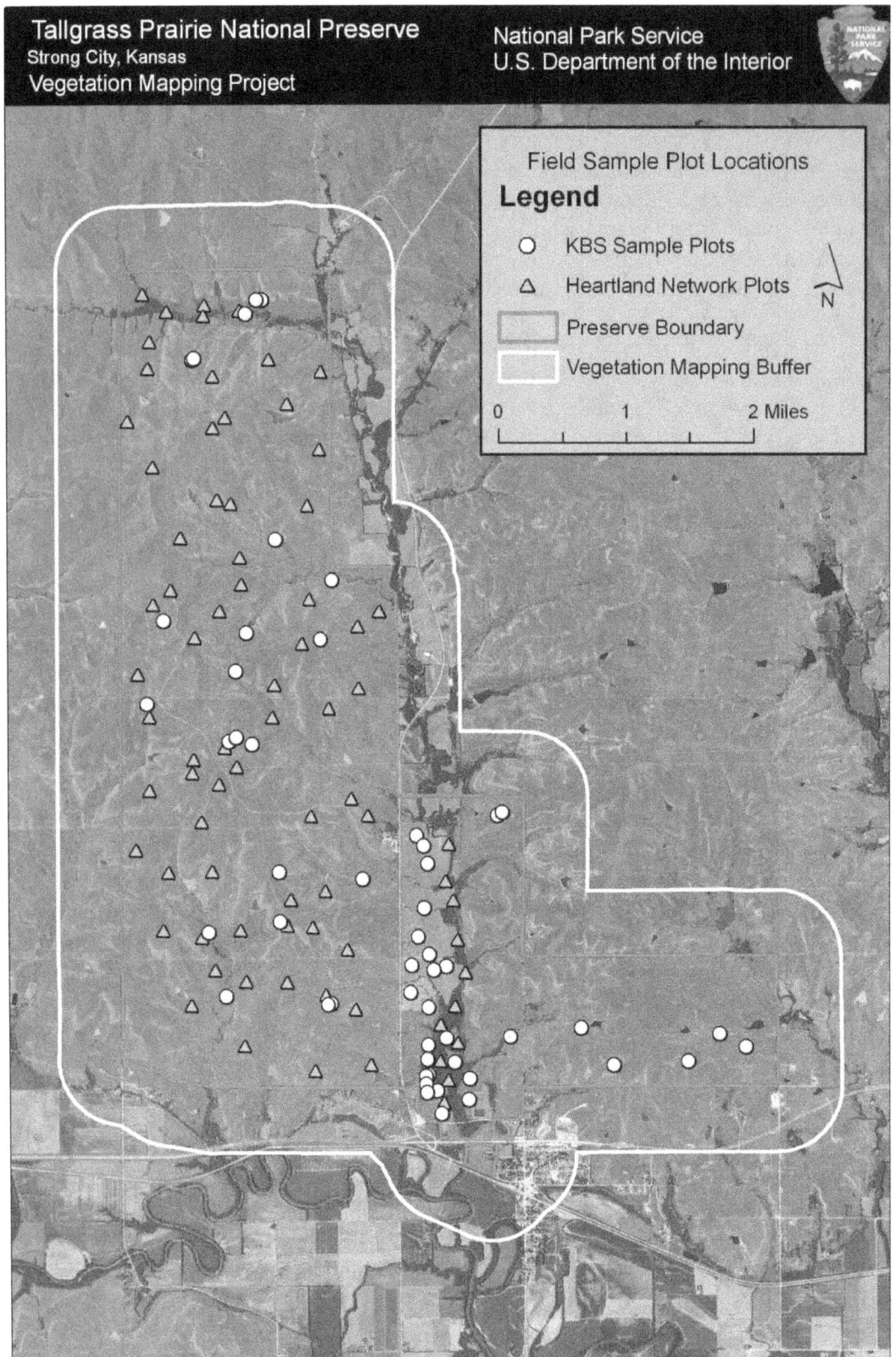

Figure 3. Locations of all vegetation plots collected at TAPR in 2008.

 Plots were assigned to categories based on similarity of vegetation. These categories were assigned names following descriptions in Lauver et al. (1999) and NatureServe Explorer (NatureServe 2006). Where the observed TAPR vegetation did not fit descriptions of natural associations described for Kansas, semi-natural and disturbed associations or alliances described for other parks were considered. In this manner, TAPR vegetation was assigned to one of ten plant associations and alliances.

Once the associations were finalized, a dichotomous key was developed by KBS for use during the Accuracy Assessment (Appendix C). The full NVC hierarchical classification and global descriptions are available in the results section. In addition, the final associations were linked to map classes for use in the photo-interpretation and mapping portions of the project.

In the future, TAPR classification plot data will be used by NatureServe and KBS to update and improve world-wide (i.e., global) descriptions of the NVC plant associations. TAPR specific (i.e., local) descriptions were written based on TAPR plot and AA data. The final TAPR classification contains six NVC vegetation classes and two Park Special vegetation classes.

Digital Imagery and Interpretation

The mapping component was initiated by photo interpretation and digitization of 4-band 2005 IKONOS imagery for the vegetation and land use classes determined through the field visit and expert knowledge of project team members. The heads-up digitization was performed at a display scale of 1:1500 to 1:2000. The digitization, evaluation, and modifications comprised an iterative and collaborative process involving the GIS analysts and the rest of the team. Preliminary maps were checked, corrected, and rechecked for boundary delineations.

Because land management practices, particularly grazing and burning, vegetation phenology, and moisture conditions reveal or mask target map features in the imagery, multiple image sources were used in an attempt to extract the most accurate and comprehensive feature classification possible. There was no one image that captured all vegetation communities and features at their peak differentiability. As noted above, a fall 2005 IKONOS image provided by the NPS served as the general basemap, with additional images used to check mapped features and make adjustments as needed. These image sources included 2003, 2004, 2005, 2006 (3-band, Red, Green, Blue), and 2008 (4-band, Red, Green, Blue, Near Infrared) USDA FSA NAIP, 2002 and 1991 USGS DOQQs, and 1938 panchromatic imagery. Two additional 4-band (Red, Green, Blue, Near Infrared) IKONOS scenes were acquired in June and September of 2008 specifically for this project. These IKONOS image acquisitions targeted specific phenological windows that were generally not covered by other imagery.

The 4-band imagery can be displayed as natural color (Red, Green, Blue) or color infrared imagery. Color infrared is often called false-color because the objects that are normally red appear green, green objects (except vegetation) appear blue, and "infrared" objects appear red. Because healthy green vegetation is a very strong reflector of infrared radiation, and appears bright red in color infrared imagery, it helps tremendously in vegetation mapping efforts. By using color infrared imagery, subtle differences between cool and warm season grasses, wetland vegetation and deciduous trees are apparent and can be accurately delineated.

Geologic strata data layers provided by the Kansas Geological Survey, generalized to shale and limestone, also served as a reference for indentifying zones where thin soiled tallgrass prairie might be present (Sawin, B.S. 2008).

Polygons were assigned map class number and name. The vegetation community polygons and other related and supporting data were then incorporated into a geodatabase format.

Accuracy Assessment

Once the vegetation layer was finalized, the accuracy assessment (AA) was conducted. Typically in mapping exercises both thematic or attribute map accuracy and the positional or polygon line accuracy are considered. In the case of the USGS-NPS National Vegetation Mapping Program, however, the positional accuracy is usually omitted since rarely does vegetation split on discrete edges that can be positively located in the field. The subjectivity involved in this effort plus the high resolution and accuracy of the NAIP and IKONOS basemaps usually allows for the assumption that all products derived from them are well within National Map Accuracy Standards for 1:12,000-scale maps (±30 feet).

The thematic accuracy of the vegetation map was assessed following the standards provided by the USGS-NPS National Vegetation Mapping Program's Accuracy Assessment Procedures manual (TNC et al. 1994). Assessment included a four step process consisting of a sample design, sample site selection, data collection and data analysis. The design of the AA process followed the five possible scenarios provided in the field manual with stratified random targets placed in each map class based on their respective frequency and abundance (Table 1).

These parameters were loaded into a GIS program along with the vegetation layer. Hawth's Analysis Tools for ArcGIS (Beyer 2004) was used to pick the random target locations and also buffer them 10 meters from any polygon boundary and 50 meters from any other point. Being able to choose minimum distance to polygon boundaries helped to minimize confusion and accounted for the horizontal error typically encountered in common GPS receivers (±5 m). The resulting target locations were restricted to the authorized boundaries of TAPR due to private land access constraints.

Once the target locations were selected they were downloaded to Garmin or Trimble GPS receivers and investigators walked to the AA points to complete the assessment. During the course of the field work, the estimated position error readings on GPS receivers ranged from 1-7 meters. KBS botanists were provided with draft field maps, map unit definitions, and a key to the associations and alliances (Appendix C). In July 2009, KBS botanists traveled to 132 AA target sites and determined the vegetation association using the field key (Figure 4). At each target they recorded vegetation data on an AA form. They also recorded height and cover of vegetative strata, environmental data, and percent canopy cover of the major species (see AA point form in Appendix D). A rationale for the choice of dominant association was noted when the decision was not clear cut.

Twenty of these points represented springs and seeps, which are not included in the vegetation classification layer. The data recorded on the field forms were subsequently entered into the PLOTS database and reviewed for data entry errors by Kansas Natural Heritage Inventory staff. The results were imported from the database into a GIS layer where they were visually compared in two stages to the vegetation map coverage. The first step was to compare the AA points to the original target locations to check for erroneous points. However, no GPS receiver or location errors were observed.

Table 1. Target number of AA samples per map class based on number of polygons and area.

Scenario	Description	Polygons in class	Area occupied by class	Recommended number of samples in class
Scenario A:	The class is abundant. It covers more than 50 hectares of the total area and consists of at least 30 polygons. In this case, the recommended sample size is 30.	>30	>50 ha	30
Scenario B:	The class is relatively abundant. It covers more than 50 hectares of the total area but consists of fewer than 30 polygons. In this case, the recommended sample size is 20. The rationale for reducing the sample size for this type of class is that sample sites are more difficult to find because of the lower frequency of the class.	<30	>50 ha	20
Scenario C:	The class is relatively rare. It covers less than 50 hectares of the total area but consists of more than 30 polygons. In this case, the recommended sample size is 20. The rationale for reducing the sample size is that the class occupies a small area. At the same time, however, the class consists of a considerable number of distinct polygons that are possibly widely distributed. The number of samples therefore remains relatively high because of the high frequency of the class.	>30	<50 ha	20
Scenario D:	The class is rare. It has more than 5 but fewer than 30 polygons and covers less than 50 hectares of the area. In this case, the recommended number of samples is 5. The rationale for reducing the sample size is that the class consists of small polygons and the frequency of the polygons is low. Specifying more than 5 sample sites will therefore probably result in multiple sample sites within the same (small) polygon. Collecting 5 sample sites will allow an accuracy estimate to be computed, although it will not be very precise.	5-30	<50 ha	5
Scenario E:	The class is very rare. It has fewer than 5 polygons and occupies less than 50 hectares of the total area. In this case, it is recommended that the existence of the class be confirmed by a visit to each sample site. The rationale for the recommendation is that with fewer than 5 sample sites (assuming 1 site per polygon) no estimate of level of confidence can be established for the sample (the existence of the class can only be confirmed through field checking).	<5	<50 ha	Visit all and confirm

Table 2. Summary of the AA statistics used at TAPR.

Statistic	Description
User's Accuracy	The fraction of the accuracy assessment observations in a map class that were found to have the correct vegetation class in the field.
Producer's Accuracy	The fraction of the accuracy assessment observations in a vegetation class in the field that were found to be mapped correctly.
Overall Accuracy	The fraction of accuracy assessment observations within all map classes that were correctly mapped.
Kappa Index	Another measure of overall accuracy, which takes into account the probability that mapped polygons will be correct due to random chance.

The second review step involved comparing the vegetation classification assigned by the field botanists to the vegetation classification assigned to the mapped polygon. If a mismatch was found, the mapped polygon would be corrected.

In the case of TAPR, the AA process was streamlined using methods developed from previous studies at Rocky Mountain National Park (Salas et al. 2004) and Wupatki National Monument (Hansen et al. 2004). All of the statistics and calculations used to analyze these data are described at length in the program manuals (TNC et al. 1994) and are summarized in Table 2. Final assessments for each point were recorded using an error matrix.

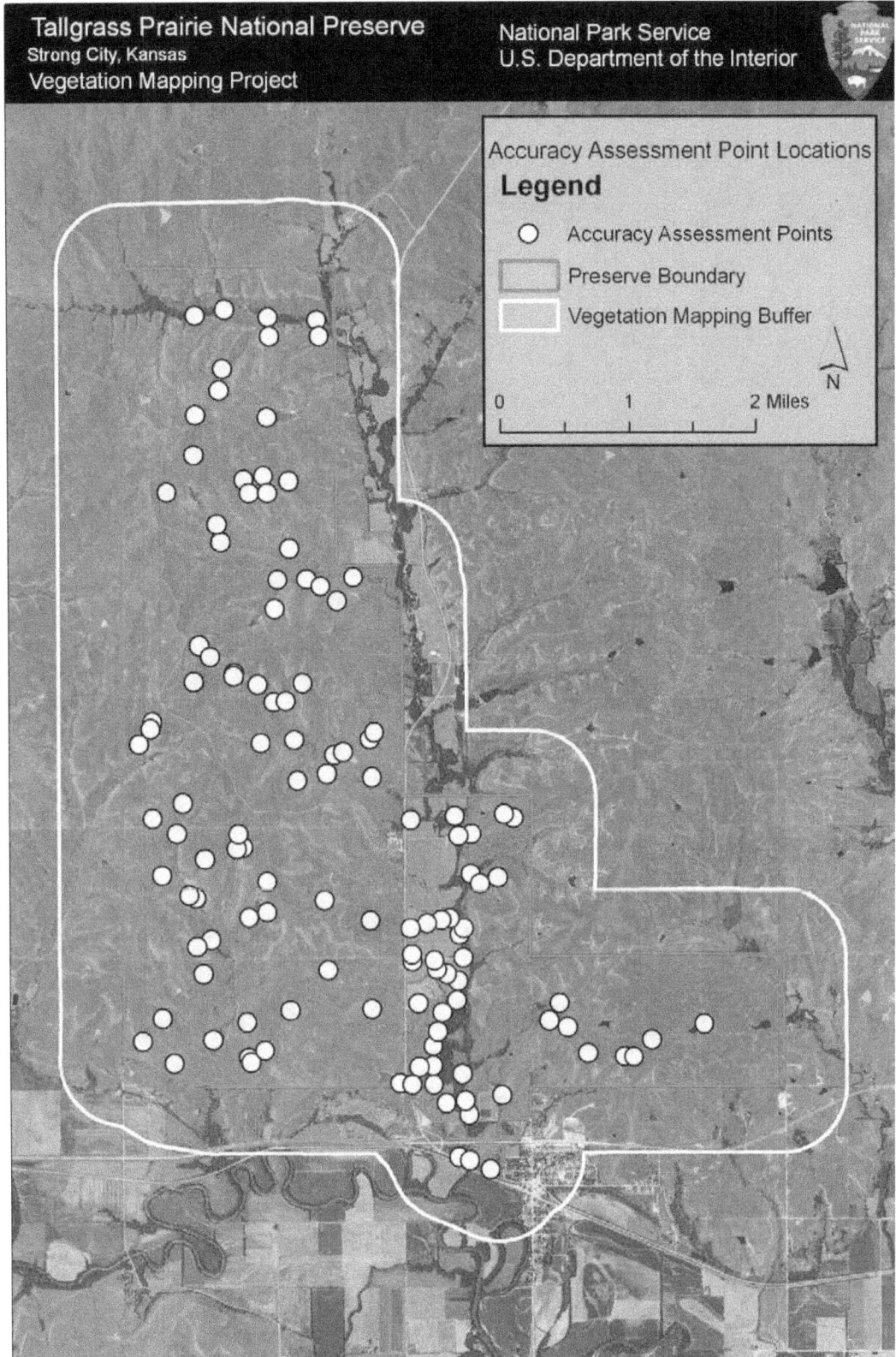

Figure 4. Locations of all accuracy assessment points collected at TAPR in 2009.

Results

Vegetation Classification
The final classification for TAPR resulted in eight vegetation classes, six of which had NVC descriptors. The other two classes, restored prairie and weedy vegetation, were considered park specific classifications. The classification results reflect both the moderate amount of diversity of vegetation in the park and a respectably high number of native species. During the sampling efforts a total of 322 species were recorded (Appendix E).

Digital Imagery and Interpretation
For TAPR, 12 map units were developed and directly matched to corresponding plant associations and land-use classes (Table 3). The types included eight vegetation based map units and four land-use classes.

Vegetation Map
Just over 18,800 acres including 10,894 acres in the authorized boundary of TAPR and an additional 7,911 acres in the environs were mapped using 12 map classes (Figure 5). This included four land cover classes and eight vegetation classes. Native Tallgrass Prairie (*Andropogon gerardii - Sorghastrum nutans - Schizachyrium scoparium* Flint Hills Herbaceous Vegetation) was the most abundant map unit in terms of area, covering 13,758 acres (5,568 hectares) or about 73% of the project area. In terms of frequency, Rocky Mixed Prairie (*Schizachyrium scoparium - Bouteloua curtipendula - Bouteloua gracilis* Central Plains Herbaceous Vegetation) was most abundant with 286 polygons. Frequencies for each map unit (i.e., number of polygons) and acreage per map unit are listed in Table 3.

The standard minimum mapping unit for NPS vegetation mapping projects is defined as 0.5 hectare. The average area of polygons for this project was 33.0 acres (13.4 hectares).

Accuracy Assessment
The 2009 accuracy assessment effort yielded 112 points that were distributed throughout TAPR; no points were sampled in the environs due to access constraints.

During analysis of the AA points, a GIS point file was created from the AA point coordinates recorded in the field. These were then overlaid on the vegetation map and a comparison of the final AA field call versus the vegetation polygon label was conducted.

Examination of the final error matrix (Appendix A) shows an overall accuracy of 92.0%. Only one map class, cropland, fell below the 80% standard due to its low frequency and low sample size. Areas of confusion occurred between similar vegetation types. Confusion occurred between bur oak forest, successional forest, and wet ravine vegetation, which all had significant overlap in species and were sometimes difficult to distinguish from aerial imagery.

Table 3. Map units identified at TAPR, with their total frequency and acreage.

NVC Identifier	Common Name	Scientific Name / Description	Frequency	Acres	Hectares
Forest and Woodlands					
CEGL002053	Bur Oak Woodland	Quercus macrocarpa / Andropogon gerardii / Hesperostipa spartea Woodland	28	509.8	206.3
CEGL002014	Successional Forest	Fraxinus pennsylvanica / Ulmus spp. / Celtis occidentalis Forest	29	409.0	165.5
Herbaceous Vegetation					
CEGL002201	Native Tallgrass Prairie	Andropogon gerardii - Sorghastrum nutans - Schizachyrium scoparium Flint Hills Herbaceous Vegetation	29	13,758.1	5,567.7
CEGL002246	Rocky Mixed Prairie	Schizachyrium scoparium - Bouteloua curtipendula - Bouteloua gracilis Central Plains Herbaceous Vegetation	286	1,351.6	547.0
CEGL002223	Wet Ravine Vegetation	Spartina pectinata - Eleocharis spp. - Carex spp. Herbaceous Vegetation	21	285.7	115.6
(No assigned code)	Restored Prairie	Planted Semi-natural Restored Tallgrass Prairie, areas that were restored to a tallgrass prairie mix of species	6	97.6	39.5
(No assigned code)	Weedy	Areas of disturbed vegetation, former feedlot	6	319.6	129.3
CEGL005264	Smooth Brome	Bromus inermis - (Pascopyrum smithii) Semi-natural Herbaceous Vegetation	23	559.4	226.4
Land Use/Land Cover					
(No assigned code)	Cropfields	Cultivated fields	42	653.8	264.6
(No assigned code)	Developed Land	Buildings and adjacent lands	24	449.8	182.0
(No assigned code)	Ponds/Water Bodies	Man-made impoundments	73	135.8	55.0
(No assigned code)	Roadways	Highways, county roads, and rights-of-way	2	274.6	111.1
Total Land Use/Land Cover			164	2,073.4	839.1
Total Natural Vegetation			405	16,731.4	6,771.0
Totals			**569**	**18,804.8**	**7,610.0**

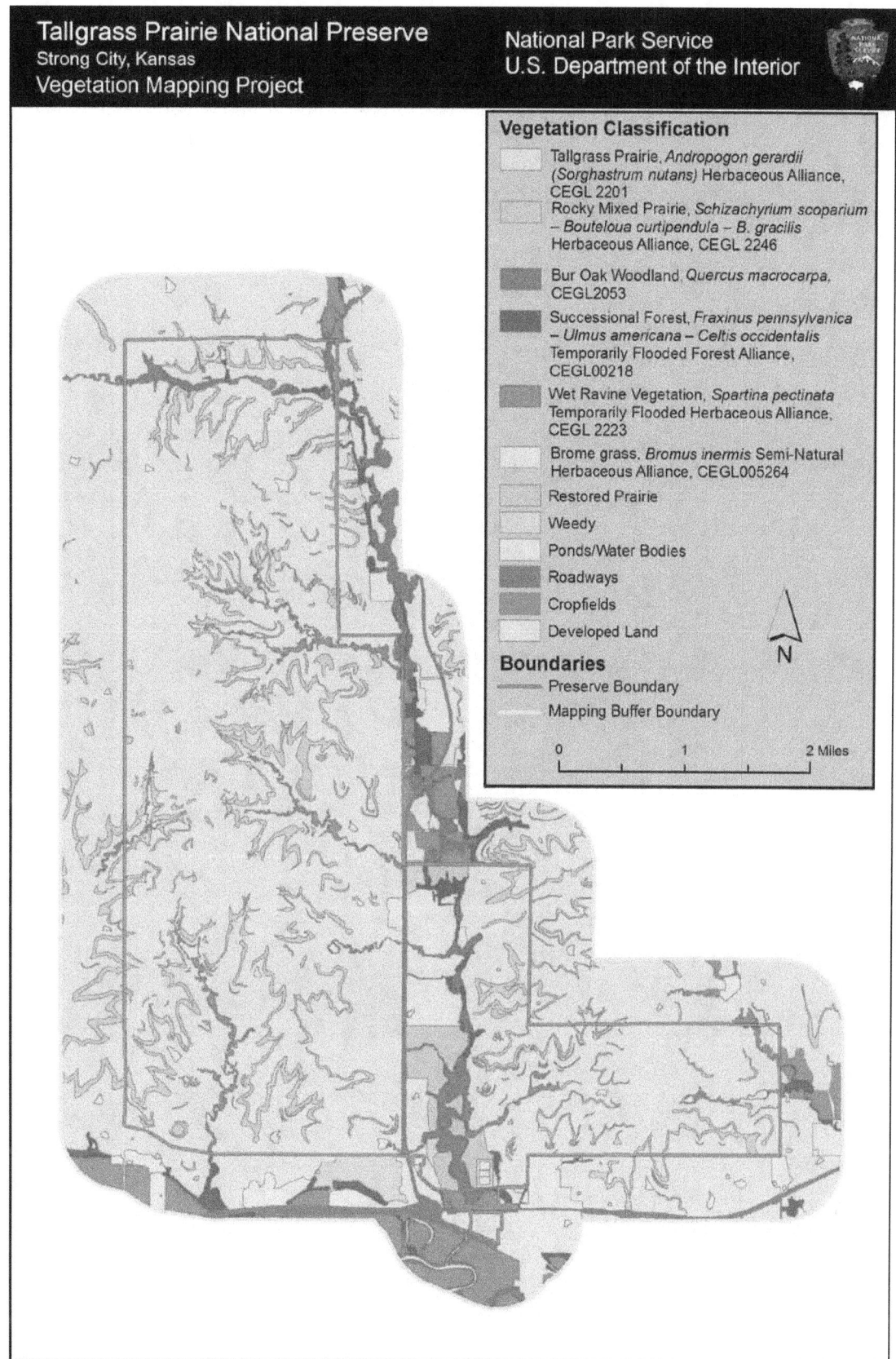

Figure 5. Vegetation map of Tallgrass Prairie National Preserve and environs.

Vegetation Associations

(note additional data and explanation can be found at NatureServe, see:
http://www.natureserve.org/explorer/servlet/NatureServe?init=Ecol

Mapped Unit Name: **Bur Oak Woodland**
Common Name: Western Tallgrass Bur Oak Woodland
Scientific Name: *Quercus macrocarpa / Andropogon gerardii - Hesperostipa spartea*
Woodland
Bur Oak / Big Bluestem - Porcupine Grass Woodland
NVC Identifier: CEGL002053

Figure 6. Bur Oak Woodland at Tallgrass Prairie National Preserve, July 2009.

Global Summary: This bur oak woodland community (Figure 6) is associated with the floodplains of rivers and streams in the central-western tallgrass region of the midwestern United States. Stands occur on gentle to steep slopes with silt or loam soils. Soils are well-drained to moderately well-drained, sometimes shallow (0-40 cm), and formed from loess or glacial till. The overstory of this community is open and dominated by *Quercus macrocarpa* (bur oak). *Quercus muehlenbergii* (chinkapin oak) can be a common associate. Shrubs are absent to common, and include *Cornus drummondii* (roughleaf dogwood), *Ceanothus herbaceus* (New Jersey tea), *Corylus americana* (American hazelnut), *Prunus americana* (American plum), *Rhus glabra* (smooth sumac), *Ribes missouriense* (Missouri gooseberry), *Symphoricarpos occidentalis* (western snowberry), and *Zanthoxylum americanum* (common pricklyash). The herbaceous

19

stratum can be similar to dry prairie. It includes the grasses *Andropogon gerardii* (big bluestem), *Schizachyrium scoparium* (little bluestem), *Sorghastrum nutans* (Indiangrass), *Sporobolus heterolepis* (prairie dropseed), and *Hesperostipa spartea* (porcupinegrass), as well as *Maianthemum stellatum* (starry false lily of the valley), *Monarda fistulosa* (wild bergamot), and *Solidago canadensis* (Canada goldenrod). In the past, periodic fires kept the canopy from closing. Where fire regimes have been disrupted, this community often begins to succeed to other, more closed oak types.

Global Environmental Description: This community occurs near floodplains and on gently sloping to steep upland mesic sites especially within 30 km of the Missouri River but possibly along other rivers. In Nebraska it may have been most abundant in the southeast because conditions are most suitable for tree growth there. The soils on which this community occurs are silt or loam, shallow to deep, with a pH range from 5.6-7.3. The soils of this community are moderately well-drained to well-drained. The parent material is loess or glacial till (Nelson 1987, Lauver et al. 1999, Steinauer and Rolfsmeier 2000).

Global Vegetation Description: The overstory of this community is open and dominated by *Quercus macrocarpa* (bur oak). *Quercus muehlenbergii* (chinkapin oak) can be a common associate. Shrubs are absent to common and include *Cornus drummondii* (roughleaf dogwood), *Ceanothus herbaceus* (New Jersey tea), *Corylus americana* (American hazelnut), *Prunus americana* (American plum), *Rhus glabra* (smooth sumac), *Ribes missouriense* (Missouri gooseberry), *Symphoricarpos occidentalis* (western snowberry), and *Zanthoxylum americanum* (common pricklyash). The herbaceous stratum can be similar to dry prairie. It includes the grasses *Andropogon gerardii* (big bluestem), *Schizachyrium scoparium* (little bluestem), *Sorghastrum nutans* (Indiangrass), *Sporobolus heterolepis* (prairie dropseed), and *Hesperostipa spartea* (porcupinegrass), as well as *Maianthemum stellatum* (starry false lily of the valley), *Monarda fistulosa* (wild bergamot), and *Solidago canadensis* (Canada goldenrod). In the past, periodic fires kept the canopy from closing. Where fire regimes have been disrupted, this community often begins to succeed to other, more closed oak types (Nelson 1987, Lauver et al. 1999, Steinauer and Rolfsmeier 2000).

Most Abundant Species:

Table 4. Overstory Tree Species (DBH>15 cm) within Bur Oak Woodland. (Data collected by Heartland Inventory and Monitoring Program, n=10 plots).

Scientific Name	Common Name	Total Trees
Celtis occidentalis	common hackberry	10
Fraxinus americana	white ash	3
Platanus occidentalis	American sycamore	3
Carya texana	black hickory	2
Fraxinus pennsylvanica	green ash	1
Gymnocladus dioicus	Kentucky coffeetree	1
Populus deltoides	eastern cottonwood	1
Quercus macrocarpa	bur oak	1
Tilia americana	American basswood	1
Ulmus americana	American elm	1
Ulmus rubra	slippery elm	1

Global Conservation Status Rank & Reasons: G2G3. This community has been highly degraded in the mesic sites where it occurred historically. Bur oak woodlands and forests have recently spread upslope into drier areas in the absence of fires. Sites do occur in Missouri in association with loess hill prairies, but are not tracked for conservation purposes because of low quality (M. Leahy pers. comm. 1999).

Mapped Unit Name: ***Successional Forest***

Common Name: Central Green Ash - Elm - Hackberry Forest

Scientific Name: *Fraxinus pennsylvanica - Ulmus* spp. *- Celtis occidentalis* Forest
Green Ash - Elm species - Common Hackberry Forest

NVC Identifier: CEGL002014

Figure 7. Successional Forest at Tallgrass Prairie National Preserve, July 2009.

Global Summary: This community (Figure 7) is found in the central United States along upper floodplain terraces of rivers and streams and in upland ravine bottoms. Soils are moderately well-drained to poorly drained. Tree canopies are dominated by *Fraxinus pennsylvanica* (green ash), *Celtis occidentalis* (common hackberry), and *Ulmus americana* (American elm). Other tree species that may be present include *Juglans nigra* (black walnut), *Tilia americana* (American basswood), *Acer saccharinum* (silver maple), and *Populus deltoides* (eastern cottonwood). *Ulmus rubra* (slippery elm) can be part of the subcanopy. The shrub layer in the western part of the range includes *Cornus drummondii* (roughleaf dogwood), *Ribes missouriense* (Missouri gooseberry), *Symphoricarpos occidentalis* (western snowberry), and *Zanthoxylum americanum* (common pricklyash), as well as woody vines, such as *Parthenocissus vitacea* (woodbine), *Smilax tamnoides* (bristly greenbrier), *Toxicodendron radicans* (eastern poison-ivy), and *Vitis riparia* (riverbank grape). The herbaceous layer in the western part of its range includes *Elymus virginicus* (Virginia wildrye), *Festuca subverticillata* (nodding fescue), *Galium aparine* (stickywilly), *Geum canadense* (white avens), and *Laportea canadensis* (Canadian woodnettle).

Global Environmental Description: Stands occur along upper floodplain terraces of rivers and streams and in upland ravine bottoms. Soils are moderately well-drained to poorly drained.

Global Vegetation Description: The vegetation has an open to closed tree canopy that is dominated by *Fraxinus pennsylvanica* (green ash), *Celtis occidentalis* (common hackberry), and *Ulmus americana* (American elm). Other tree species that may be present include *Juglans nigra* (black walnut), *Tilia americana* (American basswood), *Acer saccharinum* (silver maple), and *Populus deltoides* (eastern cottonwood). *Ulmus rubra* (slippery elm) can be part of the subcanopy. The shrub layer in the western part of the range includes *Cornus drummondii* (roughleaf dogwood), *Ribes missouriense* (Missouri gooseberry), *Symphoricarpos occidentalis* (western snowberry), and *Zanthoxylum americanum* (common pricklyash), as well as woody vines, such as *Parthenocissus vitacea* (woodbine), *Smilax tamnoides* (bristly greenbrier), *Toxicodendron radicans* (eastern poison-ivy), and *Vitis riparia* (riverbank grape). The herbaceous layer in the western part of the range includes *Elymus virginicus* (Virginia wildrye), *Festuca subverticillata* (nodding fescue), *Galium aparine* (stickywilly), *Geum canadense* (white avens), and *Laportea canadensis* (Canadian woodnettle) (Steinauer and Rolfsmeier 2000).

Most Abundant Species:

Table 5. Overstory Tree Species (DBH>15 cm) within Successional Forest. (Data collected by the Heartland Network breeding bird monitoring (n=4 plots).

Scientific Name	Common Name	Total Trees
Celtis occidentalis	common hackberry	9
Fraxinus americana	white ash	1
Robinia pseudoacacia	black locust	1
Ulmus americana	American elm	1
Ulmus rubra	slippery elm	1

Global Conservation Status Rank & Reasons: G3G5.

Mapped Unit Name: **Native Tallgrass Prairie**

Common Name: Flint Hills Tallgrass Prairie

Scientific Name: *Andropogon gerardii - Sorghastrum nutans - Schizachyrium scoparium*
Flint Hills Herbaceous Vegetation
Big Bluestem - Yellow Indiangrass - Little Bluestem Flint Hills
Herbaceous Vegetation

NVC Identifier: CEGL002201

Figure 8. Native Tallgrass Prairie at Tallgrass Prairie National Preserve, July 2009.

Global Summary: This tallgrass prairie grassland (Figure 8) is found in the Flint Hills region of the central United States. Stands occur on shallow to deep silt, loam, and clay soils. It can be somewhat poorly drained to somewhat excessively drained. This community has a dense cover of tall grasses with a moderate to high diversity of forbs. Dominant grasses are *Andropogon gerardii* (big bluestem), *Sorghastrum nutans* (Indiangrass), and *Schizachyrium scoparium* (little bluestem). *Bouteloua curtipendula* (sideoats grama), *Panicum virgatum* (switchgrass), and *Sporobolus compositus* (composite dropseed) are common, but less abundant, members of this community. Typical forbs include *Symphyotrichum ericoides* (white heath aster), *Helianthus grosseserratus* (sawtooth sunflower), *Lespedeza capitata* (roundhead lespedeza), *Solidago* (goldenrod) spp., and *Viola pedatifida* (prairie violet). Shrubs, such as *Amorpha canescens* (leadplant), and trees are usually infrequent, but can be more common near watercourses.

Global Environmental Description: This community is found on shallow to deep silt, loam, and clay soils. It can be somewhat poorly drained to somewhat excessively drained. The parent material is calcareous clayey shale, limestone, cherty limestone, or interbedded limestone and clayey shale (Lauver et al. 1999).

Global Vegetation Description: This community has a dense cover of tall grasses with a moderate to high diversity of forbs. Dominant grasses are *Andropogon gerardii* (big bluestem), *Sorghastrum nutans* (Indiangrass), and *Schizachyrium scoparium* (little bluestem). *Bouteloua curtipendula* (sideoats grama), *Panicum virgatum* (switchgrass), and *Sporobolus compositus* (composite dropseed) are common, but less abundant, members of this community. Typical forbs include *Symphyotrichum ericoides* (white heath aster), *Helianthus grosseserratus* (sawtooth sunflower), *Lespedeza capitata* (roundhead lespedeza), *Psoralidium tenuiflorum* (slimflower scurfpea), *Solidago* (goldenrod) spp., and *Viola pedatifida* (prairie violet). Shrubs, such as *Amorpha canescens* (leadplant), and trees are usually infrequent, but can be more common near watercourses (Lauver et al. 1999).

Most Abundant Species:

Table 6. Average percent cover of the top twenty most common species in plots within Native Tallgrass Prairie. (Data collected by the Heartland Network in 2008, n=23 plots.)

Scientific Name	Common Name	Average % Cover
Schizachyrium scoparium	little bluestem	23.83
Andropogon gerardii	big bluestem	12.25
Sorghastrum nutans	Indiangrass	9.04
Amphiachyris dracunculoides	prairie broomweed	6.22
Sporobolus compositus	composite dropseed	3.13
Buchloe dactyloides	buffalograss	2.93
Panicum virgatum	switchgrass	2.57
Bouteloua curtipendula	sideoats grama	2.09
Carex spp.	sedge	1.83
Ambrosia psilostachya	Cuman ragweed	1.72
Artemisia ludoviciana	white sagebrush	1.55
Lespedeza violacea	violet lespedeza	0.92
Oxalis spp.	woodsorrel	0.86
Bouteloua hirsuta	hairy grama	0.86
Oxalis violacea	violet woodsorrel	0.82
Bouteloua gracilis	blue grama	0.75
Callirhoe alcaeoides	light poppymallow	0.73
Dichanthelium spp.	rosette grass	0.67
Panicum capillare	witchgrass	0.62

Global Conservation Status Rank & Reasons: G4.

Mapped Unit Name: Rocky Mixed Prairie
Common Name: Central Great Plains Little Bluestem Prairie
Scientific Name: *Schizachyrium scoparium - Bouteloua curtipendula - Bouteloua gracilis*
                         Central Plains Herbaceous Vegetation
                         Little Bluestem - Sideoats Grama - Blue Grama Central Plains Herbaceous
                         Vegetation
NVC Identifier: CEGL 002246

Figure 9. Rocky Mixed Prairie at Tallgrass Prairie National Preserve, July 2009.

Global Summary: This little bluestem - sideoats grama grassland community (Figure 9) is found in the south-central Great Plains of the United States. Stands occur on level to moderately sloping uplands, but are more likely to be on steep ravine slopes. The loam, clay loam, silty loam, or silty soils are usually formed over limestone. They are shallow to moderately deep, well-drained, and usually contain a substantial amount of rock fragments. The vegetation often forms two layers, a shorter layer of grasses and a taller layer of mixed grasses and forbs. Cover is moderately dense to dense in most stands. The vegetation is characteristically dominated by three species, *Schizachyrium scoparium* (little bluestem), *Bouteloua curtipendula* (sideoats grama), and *Bouteloua gracilis* (blue grama). The first two are mid grasses and the latter is a short grass. *Schizachyrium scoparium* (little bluestem) is often the tallest dominant grass, reaching 0.5-0.8 m in Oklahoma. *Andropogon gerardii* (big bluestem), *Sporobolus cryptandrus* (sand dropseed), and *Sorghastrum nutans* (Indiangrass) are present, especially on lower slopes. The short grasses *Buchloe dactyloides* (buffalograss) and *Bouteloua hirsuta* (hairy grama) grow on upper slopes and level ground. Forbs include *Ambrosia psilostachya* (Cuman ragweed),

Dalea enneandra (nineanther prairie clover), *Echinacea angustifolia* (blacksamson echinacea), *Liatris punctata* (dotted blazing star), *Calylophus serrulatus* (yellow sundrops), and *Psoralidium tenuiflorum* (slimflower scurfpea).

Global Environmental Description: This community is primarily found on level to moderately sloping uplands, but is more likely to be on steep ravine slopes in western Kansas (Kuchler 1974). The loam, clay loam, silty loam, or silty soils usually formed over limestone. They are shallow to moderately deep, well-drained, and usually contain a substantial amount of rock fragments (Heitschmidt et al. 1970, Johnston 1987).

Global Vegetation Description: The vegetation in this community often forms two layers, a shorter layer of grasses and a taller layer of mixed grasses and forbs (Kuchler 1974). Cover is moderately dense to dense in most stands (Weaver and Albertson 1956). The vegetation is characteristically dominated by three species, *Schizachyrium scoparium* (little bluestem), *Bouteloua curtipendula* (sideoats grama), and *Bouteloua gracilis* (blue grama). The first two are mid grasses and the latter is a short grass. *Schizachyrium scoparium* (little bluestem) is often the tallest dominant grass, reaching 0.5-0.8 m in Oklahoma (Bruner 1931). *Andropogon gerardii* (big bluestem), *Sporobolus cryptandrus* (sand dropseed), and *Sorghastrum nutans* (Indiangrass) are present, especially on lower slopes. The short grasses *Buchloe dactyloides* (buffalograss) and *Bouteloua hirsuta* (hairy grama) grow on upper slopes and level ground. Forbs include *Ambrosia psilostachya* (Cuman ragweed), *Dalea enneandra* (nineanther prairie clover), *Echinacea angustifolia* (blacksamson echinacea), *Liatris punctata* (dotted blazing star), *Calylophus serrulatus* (yellow sundrops), and *Psoralidium tenuiflorum* (slimflower scurfpea).

Most Abundant Species:

Table 7. Average percent cover of the top twenty most common species in plots within Rocky Mixed Prairie. (Data collected by KBS in 2008, n=10 plots.)

Scientific Name	Common Name	Average % Cover
Andropogon gerardii	big bluestem	40.50
Bouteloua hirsuta	hairy grama	5.90
Bouteloua curtipendula	sideoats grama	4.21
Amorpha canescens	leadplant	3.40
Schizachyrium scoparium	little bluestem	2.41
Panicum virgatum	switchgrass	2.20
Dalea purpurea	purple prairie clover	2.14
Rhus glabra	smooth sumac	1.80
Psoralidium tenuiflorum	slimflower scurfpea	1.71
Sorghastrum nutans	Indiangrass	1.61
Vernonia baldwinii	Baldwin's ironweed	1.32
Ambrosia psilostachya	Cuman ragweed	1.03
Euthamia gymnospermoides	Texas goldentop	1.03
Artemisia ludoviciana	white sagebrush	0.32
Sporobolus compositus	composite dropseed	0.32
Tragia betonicifolia	betonyleaf noseburn	0.32
Baptisia australis	blue wild indigo	0.20
Monarda fistulosa	wild bergamot	0.20
Croton monanthogynus	prairie tea	0.14

Scientific Name	Common Name	Average % Cover
Hymenopappus scabiosaeus	Carolina woollywhite	0.13

Global Rank & Reasons: G2G4. The total number of occurrences is unknown. Seven have been documented in Kansas, where the community is ranked S2(?). Although no other occurrences have been documented, the community is also reported in Oklahoma (S?), where it may be more common.

Mapped Unit Name: ***Wet Ravine Vegetation***
Common Name: Southern Great Plains Cordgrass Wet Prairie
Scientific Name: *Spartina pectinata - Eleocharis* spp. - *Carex* spp. Herbaceous Vegetation
Prairie Cordgrass - Spikerush species - Sedge species Herbaceous
Vegetation
NVC Identifier: CEGL002223

Figure 10. Wet Ravine at Tallgrass Prairie National Preserve, July 2009.

Global Summary: This wet grassland community (Figure 10) is found in the southern Great Plains on deep, poorly drained soils on level to nearly level sites near lakes, seeps, or alluvial lowlands. The soils are usually inundated for short periods during the year but may be saturated for much of the growing season. In northeastern, central, and western Oklahoma (i.e., excluding the Coastal Plain and the Oklahoma panhandle), this association occurs in floodplains, backswamps, and lake margins. This community is characterized by tall, dense graminoids with moderate forb diversity and few woody species. The dominant species, *Spartina pectinata* (prairie cordgrass), can form near monocultures in some locations. Common species include *Carex annectens* (yellowfruit sedge), *Carex blanda* (eastern woodland sedge), *Eleocharis* (spikerush) spp., *Juncus interior* (inland rush), *Juncus torreyi* (Torrey's rush), *Panicum virgatum* (switchgrass), *Rumex altissimus* (pale dock), and *Verbena hastata* (swamp verbena). Other characteristic species in Oklahoma include *Ammannia coccinea* (valley redstem), *Paspalum laeve* (field paspalum), *Pluchea odorata* (sweetscent), and *Vernonia baldwinii* (Baldwin's ironweed), and in Kansas include *Asclepias incarnata* (swamp milkweed), *Symphyotrichum*

29

lanceolatum (white panicle aster), *Baptisia alba var. macrophylla* (largeleaf wild indigo), *Helianthus grosseserratus* (sawtooth sunflower), and *Scirpus atrovirens* (green bulrush).

Global Environmental Description: This community is found on deep, poorly drained soils on level to nearly level sites near lakes, seeps, or alluvial lowlands (Kuchler 1974, Johnson and Knapp 1995). The soils are usually inundated for short periods during the year, but may be saturated for much of the growing season.

Global Vegetation Description: This community is characterized by tall, dense graminoids with moderate forb diversity and few woody species. The dominant species, *Spartina pectinata* (prairie cordgrass), can form near monocultures in some locations (Johnson and Knapp 1995). Other common species include *Carex annectens* (yellowfruit sedge), *Carex blanda* (eastern woodland sedge), *Eleocharis* (spikerush) spp., *Juncus interior* (inland rush), *Juncus torreyi* (Torrey's rush), *Panicum virgatum* (switchgrass), *Rumex altissimus* (pale dock), and *Verbena hastata* (swamp verbena). Other characteristic species in Oklahoma include *Ammannia coccinea* (valley redstem), *Paspalum laeve* (field paspalum), *Pluchea odorata* (sweetscent), and *Vernonia baldwinii* (Baldwin's ironweed), and in Kansas include *Asclepias incarnata* (swamp milkweed), *Symphyotrichum lanceolatum* (white panicle aster), *Baptisia alba var. macrophylla* (largeleaf wild indigo), *Helianthus grosseserratus* (sawtooth sunflower), and *Scirpus atrovirens* (green bulrush) (Lauver et al. 1999).

Most Abundant Species:

Table 8. Average percent cover of the top twenty most common species in plots within Wet Ravines. (Data collected by KBS in 2008, n=10 plots; note many areas have woody encroachment)

Scientific Name	Common Name	Average % Cover
Bromus japonicus	field brome	32.31
Amorpha fruticosa	desert false indigo	23.80
Andropogon gerardii	big bluestem	12.90
Vernonia baldwinii	Baldwin's ironweed	8.32
Paspalum pubiflorum	hairyseed paspalum	8.30
Xanthium strumarium	rough cocklebur	7.61
Ambrosia psilostachya	Cuman ragweed	6.02
Sporobolus compositus	composite dropseed	5.31
Panicum virgatum	switchgrass	3.91
Ambrosia trifida	great ragweed	3.01
Muhlenbergia sp.	muhly	2.51
Solidago canadensis	Canada goldenrod	2.21
Sorghastrum nutans	Indiangrass	1.80
Teucrium canadense	Canada germander	1.80
Spartina pectinata	prairie cordgrass	1.60
Glycyrrhiza lepidota	American licorice	1.50
Leersia oryzoides	rice cutgrass	1.50
Symphoricarpos orbiculatus	coralberry	1.41
Tripsacum dactyloides	eastern gamagrass	1.21
Euthamia gymnospermoides	Texas goldentop	1.11

Global Conservation Status Rank & Reasons: G2G4. There are probably more than 20 occurrences rangewide. Six have been documented in Kansas, where the community is ranked SU. Although no other occurrences have been documented, the community is also reported in Oklahoma (S2). It occurs in four ecoregional subsections and has moderately restrictive environmental requirements.

Mapped Unit Name: Wet Ravine Vegetation - Seeps and Springs

Common Name: Southern Great Plains Cordgrass Wet Prairie

Scientific Name: *Spartina pectinata - Eleocharis* spp. - *Carex* spp. Herbaceous Vegetation Prairie Cordgrass - Spikerush species - Sedge species Herbaceous Vegetation

NVC Identifier: CEGL002223

Note: Seeps (Figure 11) and springs were surveyed separately from wet ravines, although they are included within the same community type. Seeps and springs were mapped as point locations, acquired from the Kansas Geological Survey and were not mapped as polygons.

Figure 11. Seep at Tallgrass Prairie National Preserve, July 2009. Darker green in midground is *Eleocharis spp.,* tall seedheads are *Scirpus pendulus,* and dark brown seedheads in foreground and background are *Rumex spp.*

Table 9. Average percent cover of the top twenty most common species in plots within Seeps and Springs. (Data collected by KBS in 2008, n=10 plots.)

Scientific Name	Common Name	Average % Cover
Eleocharis spp.	spikerush	19.31
Leersia oryzoides	rice cutgrass	14.40
Spartina pectinata	prairie cordgrass	13.00
Scirpus pendulus	rufous bulrush	12.40
Scirpus atrovirens	green bulrush	10.01
Carex spp.	sedge	8.51
Rorippa nasturtium-aquaticum	watercress	8.01
Juncus torreyi	Torrey's rush	7.92
Panicum virgatum	switchgrass	3.11
Ambrosia psilostachya	Cuman ragweed	2.53
Agrimonia parviflora	harvestlice	1.50
Cyperus setigerus	lean flatsedge	1.50
Amorpha fruticosa	desert false indigo	1.20
Glyceria striata	fowl mannagrass	1.11
Ambrosia artemisiifolia	annual ragweed	1.01
Andropogon gerardii	big bluestem	1.01
Carex frankii	Frank's sedge	1.01
Boehmeria cylindrica	smallspike false nettle	1.00
Carex annectens	yellowfruit sedge	0.91
Elymus virginicus	Virginia wildrye	0.81

Mapped Unit Name: Smooth Brome
Common Name: Smooth Brome Semi-natural Grassland
Scientific Name: *Bromus inermis - (Pascopyrum smithii)* Semi-natural Herbaceous Vegetation
Smooth Brome - (Western Wheatgrass) Semi-natural Herbaceous Vegetation
NVC Identifier: CEGL005264

Global Summary: This smooth brome grassland type occurs widely throughout the northern Great Plains, in disturbed montane meadows in the Rocky Mountains, on relatively mesic sites in the semi-arid interior western United States, and perhaps more widely in the midwestern U.S. and Canada. Stands can occur in a wide variety of human-disturbed habitats, including highway rights-of-way, jeep trails, etc. The type is also widely planted for revegetating disturbed land, pasture and hay fields, and has escaped into a variety of habitats, including prairie, riparian grasslands, and mesic mountain meadows. The dominant grass is *Bromus inermis* (smooth brome), a naturalized species from Eurasia that forms moderately dense to dense stands that often develop into monocultures. Other weedy species such as *Cirsium arvense* (Canada thistle) and *Poa pratensis* (Kentucky bluegrass) may occur as well, but native species are generally less than 10% cover. Native species may include mixed-grass prairie and montane meadow grasses, such as *Pascopyrum smithii* (western wheatgrass), *Deschampsia caespitosa* (tufted hairgrass), and *Hesperostipa comata* (needle-and-thread), and sparse, scattered mesic shrubs such as *Symphoricarpos* (snowberry) spp., as well as many others. However, the native species are not conspicuous enough to identify the native plant association that could occupy the site, or the stand would be typed as such.

Global Environmental Description: This smooth brome grassland type occurs widely throughout the northern Great Plains, on relatively mesic sites in the semi-arid interior western United States, and perhaps more widely in the midwestern U.S. and Canada. Stands can occur in a wide variety of human-disturbed habitats, including highway rights-of-way, jeep trails, etc. The type is also widely planted for revegetating disturbed land, pasture and hay fields, and has escaped into a variety of habitats, including prairie, riparian grasslands, and mesic mountain meadows. This community is found at all elevational ranges with best examples occurring on mesic alluvial terraces. *Bromus inermis* (smooth brome) grows best on moist, well-drained, finer-textured loam and clay loams, not heavy clays or sand, and does not tolerate prolonged flooding, however, it does persist quite well on well-drained sandy loam derived from granitic parent material. It also occurs in foothills and plains at lower elevations on relatively mesic sites. It occurs on poorly drained sites to rapidly drained sites with fine-textured alluvial soils derived from shale formations found in Utah. This community persists because it is rhizomatous, and once seeded, with enough moisture, will persist, regardless of elevation, soil or landform.

Global Vegetation Description: This association is dominated by medium-tall (0.5-1 m) graminoids. The dominant grass is *Bromus inermis* (smooth brome), a naturalized species from Eurasia that forms moderately dense to dense stands that often develop into monocultures. Other weedy species, such as *Cirsium arvense* (Canada thistle), *Poa pratensis* (Kentucky bluegrass), and other introduced forage species, may occur as well, but native species are generally less than 10% cover. Native species may include mixed-grass prairie and montane meadow grasses, such as *Juncus balticus* (Baltic rush), *Pascopyrum smithii* (western wheatgrass), *Deschampsia caespitosa* (tufted hairgrass), and *Hesperostipa comata* (needle-and-thread), and sparse scattered mesic shrubs, such as *Artemisia tridentata ssp. wyomingensis* (Wyoming big sagebrush), *Ericameria nauseosa* (rubber rabbitbrush), and *Symphoricarpos* (snowberry) spp., and ruderal forbs, such as *Heterotheca villosa* (hairy false goldenaster), as well as many others. However, the native species are not conspicuous enough to identify the native plant association that could occupy the site, or the stand would be typed as such.

Most Abundant Species:

Table 10. Average percent cover of the top twenty most common species in plots within Smooth Brome Haymeadows. Note that all species other than Bromus inermis are under 3% cover. (Data collected by KBS in 2008, n=10 plots.)

Scientific Name	Common Name	Average % Cover
Bromus inermis	smooth brome	96.50
Erigeron annuus	eastern daisy fleabane	2.61
Convolvulus arvensis	field bindweed	2.12
Physalis pumila	dwarf groundcherry	0.52
Bromus japonicus	field brome	0.23
Solanum carolinense	Carolina horsenettle	0.12
Brickellia eupatorioides	false boneset	0.11
Setaria pumila	yellow foxtail	0.11
Conyza canadensis	Canadian horseweed	0.02
Chamaesyce sp.	sandmat	0.01
Oxalis stricta	common yellow oxalis	0.01
Panicum capillare	witchgrass	0.01
Abutilon theophrasti	velvetleaf	0.01
Amaranthus rudis	roughfruit amaranth	0.01
Ambrosia artemisiifolia	annual ragweed	0.01
Asclepias viridis	green antelopehorn	0.01
Chamaesyce nutans	eyebane	0.01
Gleditsia triacanthos	honeylocust	0.01
Mirabilis nyctaginea	heartleaf four o'clock	0.01
Rumex altissimus	pale dock	0.01

Global Conservation Status Rank & Reasons: GNA (invasive) (17-Jun-1999). This is a naturalized type from Europe and Asia, widely planted for cover, pasture, and hay, and has escaped into a variety of habitats.

Common Name: **Restored Prairie**
Scientific Name: Planted Semi-natural Restored Tallgrass Prairie, areas that were restored
to a tallgrass prairie mix of species
NVC Identifier: N/A

Figure 12. Restored Prairie at Tallgrass Prairie National Preserve, July 2008.

Global Summary: This community (Figure 12) has been defined for Tallgrass Prairie National
Preserve. At TAPR, managers are attempting to restore former brome fields and weedy areas to
tallgrass prairie. Natural vegetation of this community is found throughout the northern tallgrass
prairie region of the United States and Canada.

Environmental Description: The fields that have been re-planted with native grasses at
Tallgrass Prairie National Preserve were once plowed, and have silt-loam soils.

Vegetation Description: This is a grassland community with dense vegetation dominated by
tall grasses 1-2 m tall. The abundance of forbs has not reached the abundance found in native
Flint Hills Tallgrass Prairie. *Sorghastrum nutans* (Indiangrass) and *Bromus japonicus* (field
brome) are the most abundant grasses in this community. *Conyza canadensis* (Canadian
horseweed) and *Ambrosia artemisiifolia* (annual ragweed) are common forbs.

Most Abundant Species:

Table 11. Average percent cover of the top twenty most common species in plots within Restored Prairies. (Data collected by KBS in 2008, n=19 plots.)

Scientific Name	Common Name	Average % Cover
Sorghastrum nutans	Indiangrass	21.30
Bromus japonicus	field brome	19.52
Panicum virgatum	switchgrass	15.71
Conyza canadensis	Canadian horseweed	15.02
Andropogon gerardii	big bluestem	6.91
Tripsacum dactyloides	eastern gamagrass	6.11
Ambrosia artemisiifolia	annual ragweed	5.00
Abutilon theophrasti	velvetleaf	4.61
Mollugo verticillata	green carpetweed	4.51
Chamaesyce maculata	spotted sandmat	2.70
Setaria faberi	Japanese bristlegrass	2.60
Setaria viridis	green bristlegrass	1.71
Ambrosia trifida	great ragweed	1.70
Erigeron annuus	eastern daisy fleabane	1.61
Bouteloua curtipendula	sideoats grama	1.41
Lactuca serriola	prickly lettuce	1.32
Lactuca saligna	willowleaf lettuce	1.21
Solanum carolinense	Carolina horsenettle	1.21
Amaranthus palmeri	carelessweed	1.20
Schizachyrium scoparium	little bluestem	1.01

Common Name:	***Weedy***
Scientific Name:	Areas of disturbed vegetation, former feedlot
NVC Identifier:	N/A

Figure 13. Weedy area at Tallgrass Prairie National Preserve, July 2008.

Global Summary and Environmental Description: This community (Figure 13) has been defined for Tallgrass Prairie National Preserve. At TAPR, these are fields that were formerly plowed or used as feedlots, and have not yet been restored to Flint Hills Tallgrass Prairie.

Vegetation Description: This is a grassland community with dense vegetation dominated by tall grasses 1-2 m tall. Exotic grasses, *Bromus inermis* (smooth brome) and *Bromus japonicus* (field brome), are the most abundant grasses in this community. *Convolvulus arvensis* (field bindweed) and *Erigeron annuus* (eastern daisy fleabane) are common forbs.

Most Abundant Species:

Table 12. Average percent cover of the top nineteen most common species in plots within Weedy Areas. (Data collected by KBS in 2008, n=4 plots.)

Scientific Name	Common Name	Average % Cover
Bromus inermis	smooth brome	32.50
Bromus japonicus	field brome	31.26
Convolvulus arvensis	field bindweed	20.75
Ambrosia trifida	great ragweed	15.00
Conyza canadensis	Canadian horseweed	7.75
Erigeron annuus	eastern daisy fleabane	6.25
Kochia scoparia	burningbush	6.25
Rumex crispus	curly dock	3.25
Mirabilis nyctaginea	heartleaf four o'clock	2.00
Sorghum halepense	Johnsongrass	2.00
Cucurbita foetidissima	Missouri gourd	1.75
Phytolacca americana	American pokeweed	1.28
Torilis arvensis	spreading hedgeparsley	1.26
Acalypha ostryifolia	pineland threeseed mercury	1.25
Lactuca serriola	prickly lettuce	1.25
Cirsium altissimum	tall thistle	0.75
Helianthus annuus	common sunflower	0.51
Gleditsia triacanthos	honeylocust	0.50
Physalis longifolia	longleaf groundcherry	0.03

Discussion

Tallgrass Prairie National Preserve combines a unique mix of historically important structures and a significant example of native tallgrass prairie.

Field Survey
The vegetation data presented in this project should be used as a baseline to build upon. New survey work in a timely manner would greatly improve both the classification and mapping efforts. Also, accessing neighboring private lands would allow new plot samples to be obtained, increasing the confidence in these types, thereby strengthening the classification.

NVC Classification
In addition to providing a highly accurate vegetation map of the park and environs, we were able to particularly focus on mapping rocky mixed prairie, a sub-community of native tallgrass prairie that is present on limestone outcrops throughout the park.

Digital Imagery and Interpretation
Multiple sources of imagery were used to digitize the vegetation map, which allowed very thorough examination of subtle vegetation characteristics and photo signatures (e.g., shadows of canopy trees). Analyzing imagery taken over multiple seasons, multiple years, and with multiple color band displays allowed us to map boundaries in fine detail and with high confidence.

Accuracy Assessment
We were able to obtain a 92.0% accuracy for map classes, and a kappa adjustment for chance agreements results in an overall accuracy of 90.6%. Our overall accuracy assessment is well above the 80% required by VMP (taking into account the 90% confidence interval). Individual accuracies also met the 80% requirement, with two exceptions:

(1) Cropland: Users' accuracy for this vegetation class is 67%, with a 90% confidence interval of 5%-128%. Of the three accuracy assessment sites mapped as cropland, one was determined to be smooth brome on the ground. Producers' accuracy is 100%, with a 90% confidence interval of 75%-125%.

(2) Central Green Ash - Elm - Hackberry Forest: Producers' accuracy for this vegetation class is 75%, with a 90% confidence interval of 44%-106%. Of the eight accuracy assessment sites classified as this category on the ground, one was mapped as wet ravine and one was mapped as bur oak forest. These three categories were sometimes difficult to distinguish from overhead imagery. Users' accuracy is 86%, with a 90% confidence interval of 57%-115%.

Future Recommendations
In summary, this project represents the best efforts put forth by a multi-disciplined team over a relatively short period in time. In order to create the best possible "long-term" vegetation classification for TAPR and the most accurate and detailed GIS layer, this project should be viewed as a place to start rather than an end product. Present and future NPS staff are encouraged to scrutinize this project, building from its strengths and bolstering its weaknesses. By keeping in mind that this project was only a snapshot in time, future efforts can help complete our understanding of the vegetation in and around TAPR and how it changes. It is the hope of the producers that the

products presented here will help focus and direct future efforts. The following recommendations are summarized below.

1. The diversity of plant species and dynamic nature of the park with respect to the agricultural aspect warrants periodic **field surveys** by experienced ecologists. The inaccessibility of private lands in the environs should be addressed by seeking permission to sample and verify the vegetation. In this way new plant associations could be discovered and existing types could be updated.

2. Remote sensing does not replace on-the-ground knowledge provided by GPS-linked plots, observations and ground verification. Time and funding limitations curtailed the amount of map **ground-truthing** performed. As opportunities arise, maps should be examined in the field by experienced crews. GPS receiver data and other GIS layers should be used to improve and update the spatial data. This map product should not be viewed as static but should be updated with more current and accurate information.

3. For monitoring purposes, **change over time** could be addressed by similar remote sensing projects. New aerial photos or NAIP imagery could be used in regular intervals to document change. Specifically, new imagery could be used to create up-to-date vegetation layers that could be used to compare changes in both individual vegetation stands and across the entire park.

4. In the future, resource management personnel could link the habitat for **species of concern** to specific associations and map units. These map units could then be used to help locate potential sites of endangered or threatened species in the field or identify areas for non-native plant removal or treatment.

Research Opportunities

Having an accurate and current vegetation classification and map presents many new and exciting research opportunities. These include expanding or linking the GIS layer to derive other information such as fire models, habitat monitoring locations, guides for rare plant surveys, and inventorying areas that likely contain exotic or invasive species. The map could be enhanced by overlaying other existing GIS layers such as geology, hydrology, elevation, and soils. In this manner complex interactions between these layers could be examined to yield important information about growth rates, regeneration after disturbance, biomass distribution, and stream morphology. Finally, through innovative analyses the vegetation layer could possibly be used as a springboard for other ecological studies such as examining how the vegetation interacts with soil chemistry, pollution, archeological sites, weather patterns, etc.

Literature Cited

Beyer, H. L. 2004. Hawth's Analysis Tools for ArcGIS. Available at http://www.spatialecology.com/htools.

Bruner, W. E. 1931. The vegetation of Oklahoma. Ecological Monographs 1:99-188.

Daubenmire, R. 1959. A canopy-coverage method of vegetational analysis. Northwest Science 33(1): 42-65.

Federal Geographic Data Committee (FGDC). 1997. Vegetation classification standard, FGDC-STD-005-1997. Available at: http://www.fgdc.gov/standards/status/sub2_1.html.

Federal Geographic Data Committee (FGDC). 1998a. Content standard for digital geospatial metadata, FGDC-STD-001-1998. Available at http://www.fgdc.gov/metadata/contstan.html.

Federal Geographic Data Committee (FGDC). 1998b. Spatial data transfer standard, FGDC-STD-002 (modified version ANSI NCITS 20:1998). Available at http://www.fgdc.gov/standards/status/textstatus.html.

Grossman D. H., D. Faber-Langendoen, A. S. Weakley, M. Anderson, P. Bourgeron, R. Crawford, K. Goodin, S. Landaal, K. Metzler, K. D. Patterson, M. Pyne, M. Reid, and L. Sneddon. 1998. International classification of ecological communities: terrestrial vegetation of the United States. Volume I, The National Vegetation Classification System: development, status, and applications. The Nature Conservancy: Arlington, VA. Available at http://www.natureserve.org/publications/library.jsp#nspubs.

Grossman, D. H., K. L. Goodin, X. Li, D. Faber-Langendoen, M. Anderson, and R. Vaughan. 1994. Establishing standards for field methods and mapping procedures. Prepared for the USGS-NPS Vegetation Mapping Program by The Nature Conservancy, Arlington VA, and Environmental Science Research Institute, Redlands, CA.

Hansen, M., J. Coles, K. Thomas, D. Cogan, M. Ried, J. VonLoh, and K. Schulz. 2004. USGS-NPS National Vegetation Mapping Program: Wupatki National Monument, Arizona; Vegetation Classification and Distribution. Final Report. U.S. Geological Survey Southwest Biological Science Center. Flagstaff, AZ.

Heitschmidt, R. K., G. K. Hulett, and G. W. Tomanek. 1970. Vegetational map and community structure of a west central Kansas prairie. Southwestern Naturalist 14(3):337-350.

James, K. M., M. D. DeBacker, G. A. Rowell, J. L. Haack and L. W. Morrison. 2009. Vegetation community monitoring protocol for the Heartland Inventory and Monitoring Network. Natural Resource Report NPS/HTLN/NRR — 2009/141. National Park Service, Fort Collins, Colorado.

Johnson, S. R., and A. K. Knapp. 1995. The influence of fire on *Spartina pectinata* wetland communities in a northeastern Kansas tallgrass prairie. Canadian Journal of Botany 73:84-90.

Johnston, B. C. 1987. Plant associations of Region Two: Potential plant communities of Wyoming, South Dakota, Nebraska, Colorado, and Kansas. R2-ECOL-87-2. USDA Forest Service, Rocky Mountain Region. Lakewood, CO. 429 pp.

Kuchler, A. W. 1974. A new vegetation map of Kansas. Ecology 55:586-604 (with map supplement).

Lauver, C. L., K. Kindscher, D. Faber-Langendoen, and R. Schneider. 1999. A classification of the natural vegetation of Kansas. The Southwestern Naturalist 44:421-443.

Leahy, M. Personal communication. 1999. Missouri Natural Heritage Database, Missouri Department of Conservation, Jefferson City.

McGregor, R. L., and T. M. Barkley, eds. 1986. Flora of the Great Plains. University Press of Kansas, Lawrence, KS.

NatureServe. 2006. NatureServe Explorer: An online encyclopedia of life [web application]. Version 4.7. NatureServe, Arlington, VA. Available at http://www.natureserve.org/explorer.

Nelson, P. W. 1987 [1985]. The terrestrial natural communities of Missouri. Missouri Natural Areas Committee, Jefferson City. 197 pp.

Peitz, D.G., G.A. Rowell, J.L. Haack, K.M. James, L.W. Morrison, and M.D. DeBacker. 2008. Breeding Bird Monitoring Protocol for the Heartland Network Inventory and Monitoring Program. Natural Resource Report NPS/HTLN/NRR- 2008/044. National Park Service, Fort Collins, Colorado.

Salas, D., J. Stevens, and K. Schulz. 2004. USGS-NPS National Vegetation Mapping Program: Rocky Mountain National Park. Final Report. U.S. Bureau of Reclamation Remote Sensing and GIS Group Technical Memorandum 8260-05-02. Denver, Colorado.

Sawin, B.S. 2008. Surficial geology of the Tallgrass Prairie National Preserve, Chase County, Kansas: Kansas Geological Survey, Map M-119A, scale 1:12,000.

Sawin, R. and R. Buchanan. 2000. Water Quality of Selected Springs--Tallgrass Prairie National Preserve, Chase County, Kansas. Kansas Geological Survey, Open-file Report 2000-01.

Steinauer, G., and S. Rolfsmeier. 2000. Terrestrial natural communities of Nebraska. Unpublished report of the Nebraska Game and Parks Commission. Lincoln, NE. 143 pp.

The Nature Conservancy (TNC). 1996. Methodology for Assessing the Utility of Existing Data for Vegetation Mapping. Arlington, VA.

The Nature Conservancy (TNC). 1997. PLOTS Database System, Version 1.1. Arlington, VA.

The Nature Conservancy (TNC) and Environmental Systems Research Institute (ESRI). 1994a. NBS/NPS Vegetation Mapping Program: Standardized National Vegetation Classification System. Prepared for the U.S. Department of the Interior, National Biological Survey and National Park Service. Washington, D.C.

The Nature Conservancy (TNC) and Environmental Systems Research Institute (ESRI). 1994b. NBS/NPS Vegetation Mapping Program: Field Methods for Vegetation Mapping. Prepared for the U.S. Department of the Interior, National Biological Survey and National Park Service. Washington, D.C.

The Nature Conservancy (TNC), Environmental Systems Research Institute, and National Center of Geographic Information and Analysis. 1994. NBS/NPS Vegetation Mapping Program: Accuracy Assessment Procedures. Prepared for the U.S. Department of the Interior, National Biological Survey and National Park Service. Washington, D.C.

U.S. Geological Survey. 1999. Map accuracy standards. Fact sheet FS-171-99 (November 1999). Web address: http://mac.usgs.gov/mac/isb/pubs/factsheets/fs17199.html.

USDA and NRCS. 2009. The PLANTS Database (http://plants.usda.gov, 19 November 2009). National Plant Data Center, Baton Rouge, LA 70874-4490 USA.

Weaver, J. E., and F. W. Albertson. 1956. Grasslands of the Great Plains: Their nature and use. Johnsen Publishing Co., Lincoln, NE. 395 pp.

Wolfenbarger and Nimz, 1996. Spring Hill Ranch, Chase County, Kansas, National Historic Landmark Nomination (March 5, 1996)

Appendix A: contingency Table for Vegetation Mapping at TAPR

Map Units	Tallgrass Prairie	Rocky Mixed Prairie	Wet Ravine	Success. Forest	Weedy	Bur Oak	Smooth Brome	Cropland	Restored Prairie	Totals	Commission Accuracy	90% Conf. Interval −	90% Conf. Interval +
Tallgrass Prairie	19	1			1					21	90%	78%	103%
Rocky Mixed Prairie	1	25								26	96%	88%	104%
Wet Ravine			14	1		1				16	88%	71%	104%
Success. Forest				6		1				7	86%	57%	115%
Weedy				1	8					9	89%	66%	112%
Bur Oak						12	1			13	92%	76%	108%
Smooth Brome							12			12	100%	96%	104%
Cropland							1	2		3	67%	5%	128%
Restored Prairie									5	5	100%	90%	110%
Totals	20	26	14	8	9	14	14	2	5				
Omission Accuracy	95%	96%	100%	75%	89%	86%	86%	100%	100%		103 Total Correct Points		
90% Conf. Level −	84%	88%	96%	44%	66%	67%	67%	75%	90%		112 Total Points		
90% Conf. Level +	106%	104%	104%	106%	112%	105%	105%	125%	110%				

Sample Data (Polygon Map Data)

Producer's Error

Overall Total Accuracy = 92.0% Overall Kappa Index = 90.6% Overall 90% Upper and Lower Confidence Interval =87.3% and 96.6%

Instructions on Using the Accuracy Assessment Contingency Table:

The contingency table or error matrix found above presents an array of numbers set out in rows and columns corresponding to a particular vegetation map unit relative to the actual vegetation type as verified on the ground. The column headings represent the vegetation classification as determined in the field and the row headings represent the vegetation classification taken from the vegetation map. The highlighted diagonal indicates the number of points assessed in the field that agree with the map label. Conversely, the inaccuracies of each map unit are described as both errors of inclusion (user's or commission errors) and errors of exclusion (producer's or omission errors). By reading across this table (i.e., rows) one can calculate the percent error of commission, or how many polygons for each map unit were incorrectly labeled when compared to the field data. By reading down the table (i.e., columns) one can calculate the percent error of omission, or how many polygons for that type were left off the map. Numbers "on the diagonal" tell the user how well the map unit was interpreted and how confident they can be in using it. Numbers "off the diagonal" yield important information about the deficiencies of the map including which types were: 1) over- mapped - commission errors on the right or 2) under-mapped - omission errors on the bottom.

Appendix B: Example of a Plot Sampling Form

IDENTIFIERS/LOCATORS

Plot Code_____
Provisional Community Name_____
State ___ Site Name_____ Local Site Name_____
Quad Name_____
GPS file name_____ Field UTM X__ __ __ __ __ __ m E   Field UTM Y__ __ __ __ __ __ __ m N
Datum_____   Error +/-_____ m *please do not complete the following information when in the field* Corrected UTM X__ __ __ __ __ __ m E Corrected UTM Y__ __ __ __ __ __ __ m N   UTM Zone_____
Project Name_____ Project Leader_____
Survey Date_____ Surveyor Lead _____Surveyors_____
Taxonomic authority _____
Directions to Plot
Plot length_____ Plot width_____ Plot area _____
Plot Photos (y/n) ___ Roll Number _____ Frame Number _____ Plot Permanent (y/n) ____
Plot representativeness

ENVIRONMENTAL DESCRIPTION

Elevation _____ Slope _____ Aspect_____
Topographic Position

Cowardan System ___Upland ___Riverine ___Palustrine ___Lacustrine	Non Tidal ___Permanently Flooded ___Semipermanently Flooded ___Saturated ___Seasonally Flooded ___Seasonally Flooded/Saturated ___Temporarily Flooded ___Intermittently Flooded	Tidal __ _____

Environmental Comments:	Soil Drainage ___ Rapidly drained ___ Well drained ___ Moderately well drained ___ Somewhat poorly drained ___ Poorly drained ___ Very poorly drained
Soil Comments	Landscape/Landform Comments

1

VEGETATION DESCRIPTION

Leaf phenology (of dominant stratum)	Leaf Type (of dominant stratum)	Physiognomic class	Cover Scale for Species		Height Scale for Strata	
Trees or Shrubs ___Evergreen ___Cold-deciduous ___Drought-deciduous ___Mixed evergreen - cold-deciduous ___Mixed evergreen - drought-deciduous Herbs ___Annual ___Perennial	___Broad-leaved ___Needle-leaved ___Microphyllous ___Graminoid ___Forb ___Pteridophyte	___Forest ___Woodland ___Shrubland ___Dwarf-shrubland ___Herbaceous ___Nonvascular ___Sparsely Vegetated	√ 1 2 3 4 5 6 7 8 9 10	Nearby 0-.01% .01-1% 1-2% 2-5% 5-10% 10-25% 25-50% 50-75% 75-95% 95-100%	01 02 03 04 05 06 07 08 09 10	<0.5 m 0.5-1m 1-2 m 2-5 m 5-10 m 10-15 m 15-20 m 20-35 m 35 - 50 m >50 m

Layer (sublayer–optional)	Height Class	Layer % Cover	Dominant and characteristic Species and Cover Class
T Tree	_____		_____
T_ _____	_____ _____		_____
T_ _____	_____ _____		_____
S Shrub	_____		_____
S_ ____	_____ _____		_____
S_ ____	_____ _____		_____
H Herbaceous	_____ _____		_____
N Nonvascular	_____ _____		_____
_ ____	_____		_____

please see above table for height and cover scales

Animal Use Evidence

Natural and Anthropogenic Disturbance Comments

Other Comments

2

50

Appendix C: Tallgrass Prairie National Preserve Dichotomous Key to Vegetation Associations

1a. Plant community dominated by trees..**2**

1b. Plant community dominated by herbaceous vegetation. If woody plants are present, they are scattered individuals or brush due to lack of recent fire...**3**

2a. Woodland or forest of mixed trees of mixed heights, and mixed ages with no old growth trees.............................
Central Green Ash – Elm – Hackberry Forest CEGL00214

2b. Forest with mix of trees, but includes old-growth bur oaks..
Western Tallgrass Bur Oak Woodland CEGL002053

3a. Dominated by planted non-native plants...**4**

3b. Dominated by native grasses and native forbs...**6**

4a. Dominated by non-native grasses and annual forbs (annual forbs >5% cover).............................**Weedy**

4b. Dominated by non-native grasses or crop; if forbs are present, <5% cover...................................**5**

5a. Planted brome grass......................**Smooth Brome grass *Bromus inermis* Semi-natural Herbaceous Alliance**

5b. Planted agricultural crops...**Cropland**

6a. Native prairie with forbs..**7**

6b. Replanted or Restored Tallgrass Prairie.................................**Planted Semi-natural Restored Tallgrass Prairie**

7a. Dominated by plants associated with wet places (*Eleocharis, Spartina, Amorpha fruticosa*)................**8**

7b. Dominated by *Andropogon gerardii*...**9**

8a. At a spring or seep..**Spring or Seep**

8b. In a riparian area near a stream...........................**Southern Great Plains Cordgrass Wet Prairie CEGL002223**

9a. Greater than 5% rock cover......................**Central Great Plains Little Bluestem Prairie CEGL002246**

9b. Less than 5% rock cover..**Flint Hills Tallgrass Prairie CEGL002201**

Appendix D: Example of an Accuracy Assessment Sampling Form

NPS Vegetation Mapping: Accuracy Assessment Form

Plot # _____   Park Code: **TAPR**   Observers: _____   Date: _____

UTM X _ _ _ _ _ _ m E   UTM Y _ _ _ _ _ _ _ m N   Zone: _____

Datum: _____   PDOP _____   Elevation _____   Waypoint: _____

Topography: _____   Slope: _____   Picture no(s): _____

	Stratum	Height (m)	% Cover of Strata	Major Species Present	% Cover of Each Species
T1	Emergent				
T2	Canopy				
T3	Subcanopy (<10 cm DBH)				
S1	Tall Shrub (2-5 m)				
S2	Short Shrub (<2m)				
H	Herbaceous				
A1	Floating Leaved Aquatic				
A2	Submerged Aquatic				
N	Nonvascular				

Comments on indicator species or rare species: _____

_____

Mapped Vegetation Association: _____

Observed Vegetation Association: _____

Comments (note influences on vegetation, difficulties with classification, etc):

Appendix E: Tallgrass Prairie National Preserve Species List

Family	Scientific Name	Common Name
Acanthaceae	*Justicia americana*	American water-willow
	Ruellia humilis	fringeleaf wild petunia
Aceraceae	*Acer negundo*	boxelder
Amaranthaceae	*Amaranthus palmeri*	carelessweed
	Amaranthus tuberculatus	roughfruit amaranth
Anacardiaceae	*Rhus aromatica*	fragrant sumac
	Rhus glabra	smooth sumac
	Toxicodendron radicans	eastern poison ivy
Apiaceae	*Cicuta maculata*	spotted water hemlock
	Lomatium foeniculaceum	desert biscuitroot
	Spermolepis inermis	Red River scaleseed
	Torilis arvensis	spreading hedgeparsley
Apocynaceae	*Apocynum cannabinum*	Indianhemp
Asclepiadaceae	*Asclepias sullivantii*	prairie milkweed
	Asclepias syriaca	common milkweed
	Asclepias tuberosa	butterfly milkweed
	Asclepias verticillata	whorled milkweed
	Asclepias viridiflora	green comet milkweed
	Asclepias viridis	green antelopehorn
Asteraceae	*Achillea millefolium*	common yarrow
	Ageratina altissima	white snakeroot
	Ambrosia artemisiifolia	annual ragweed
	Ambrosia psilostachya	Cuman ragweed
	Ambrosia trifida	great ragweed
	Amphiachyris dracunculoides	prairie broomweed
	Antennaria neglecta	field pussytoes
	Arnoglossum plantagineum	groovestem Indian plaintain
	Artemisia ludoviciana	white sagebrush
	Bidens frondosa	devil's beggartick
	Brickellia eupatorioides	false boneset
	Cirsium altissimum	tall thistle
	Cirsium undulatum	wavyleaf thistle
	Conyza canadensis	Canadian horseweed
	Echinacea angustifolia	blacksamson echinacea
	Eclipta prostrata	false daisy
	Erechtites hieraciifolia	American burnweed
	Erigeron annuus	eastern daisy fleabane
	Erigeron philadelphicus	Philadelphia fleabane
	Erigeron strigosus	prairie fleabane
	Eupatorium altissimum	tall thoroughwort
	Euthamia gymnospermoides	Texas goldentop
	Helianthus annuus	common sunflower
	Helianthus grosseserratus	sawtooth sunflower
	Helianthus maximiliani	Maximilian sunflower
	Helianthus pauciflorus	stiff sunflower

Family	Scientific Name	Common Name
	Hieracium longipilum	hairy hawkweed
	Hymenopappus scabiosaeus	Carolina woollywhite
	Iva annua	annual marshelder
	Krigia caespitosa	weedy dwarfdandelion
	Lactuca canadensis	Canada lettuce
	Lactuca saligna	willowleaf lettuce
	Lactuca serriola	prickly lettuce
	Liatris punctata	dotted blazing star
	Nothocalais cuspidata	prairie false dandelion
	Oligoneuron rigidum	stiff goldenrod
	Packera plattensis	prairie groundsel
	Ratibida columnifera	upright prairie coneflower
	Ratibida pinnata	pinnate prairie coneflower
	Rudbeckia hirta	blackeyed Susan
	Silphium integrifolium	wholeleaf rosinweed
	Silphium laciniatum	compassplant
	Solidago canadensis	Canada goldenrod
	Solidago gigantea	giant goldenrod
	Solidago missouriensis	Missouri goldenrod
	Solidago speciosa	showy goldenrod
	Symphyotrichum ericoides	white heath aster
	Symphyotrichum laeve	smooth blue aster
	Symphyotrichum lanceolatum	white panicle aster
	Symphyotrichum oblongifolium	aromatic aster
	Symphyotrichum praealtum	willowleaf aster
	Symphyotrichum sericeum	western silver aster
	Taraxacum officinale	common dandelion
	Verbesina alternifolia	wingstem
	Vernonia baldwinii	Baldwin's ironweed
	Xanthium strumarium	rough cockleburr
Boraginaceae	*Lithospermum canescens*	hoary puccoon
	Lithospermum incisum	narrowleaf stoneseed
	Myosotis verna	spring forget-me-not
	Onosmodium bejariense	soft-hair marbleseed
Brassicaceae	*Alliaria petiolata*	garlic mustard
	Camelina microcarpa	littlepod false flax
	Descurainia pinnata	western tansymustard
	Draba brachycarpa	shortpod draba
	Draba cuneifolia	wedgeleaf draba
	Draba reptans	Carolina draba
	Lepidium densiflorum	common pepperweed
	Nasturtium officinale	watercress
	Thlaspi arvense	field pennycress
Cactaceae	*Escobaria missouriensis*	Missouri foxtail cactus
	Opuntia macrorhiza	twistspine pricklypear
Campanulaceae	*Lobelia siphilitica*	great blue lobelia
	Triodanis perfoliata	clasping Venus' looking-glass

Family	Scientific Name	Common Name
Caprifoliaceae	*Sambucus nigra*	European black elderberry
	Symphoricarpos orbiculatus	coralberry
Caryophyllaceae	*Cerastium brachypodum*	shortstalk chickweed
	Dianthus armeria	Deptford pink
	Silene antirrhina	sleepy silene
	Stellaria media	common chickweed
Chenopodiaceae	*Bassia scoparia*	burningbush
	Chenopodium album	lambsquarters
Commelinaceae	*Tradescantia bracteata*	longbract spiderwort
Convolvulaceae	*Calystegia sepium*	hedge false bindweed
	Convolvulus arvensis	field bindweed
	Evolvulus nuttallianus	shaggy dwarf morning-glory
Cornaceae	*Cornus drummondii*	roughleaf dogwood
Cucurbitaceae	*Cucurbita foetidissima*	Missouri gourd
Cupressaceae	*Juniperus virginiana*	eastern redcedar
Cyperaceae	*Carex annectens*	yellowfruit sedge
	Carex austrina	southern sedge
	Carex bicknellii	Bicknell's sedge
	Carex brevior	shortbeak sedge
	Carex frankii	Frank's sedge
	Carex gravida	heavy sedge
	Carex molesta	troublesome sedge
	Carex muehlenbergii	Muhlenberg's sedge
	Carex vulpinoidea	fox sedge
	Cyperus acuminatus	tapertip flatsedge
	Cyperus esculentus	yellow nutsedge
	Cyperus lupulinus	Great Plains flatsedge
	Cyperus odoratus	fragrant flatsedge
	Cyperus setigerus	lean flatsedge
	Cyperus strigosus	strawcolored flatsedge
	Eleocharis compressa	flatstem spikerush
	Schoenoplectus tabernaemontani	softstem bulrush
	Scirpus atrovirens	green bulrush
	Scirpus pendulus	rufous bulrush
Euphorbiaceae	*Acalypha ostryifolia*	pineland threeseed mercury
	Acalypha rhomboidea	common threeseed mercury
	Acalypha virginica	Virginia threeseed mercury
	Chamaesyce maculata	spotted sandmat
	Chamaesyce nutans	eyebane
	Chamaesyce prostrata	prostrate sandmat
	Croton capitatus	hogwort
	Croton monanthogynus	prairie tea
	Euphorbia dentata	toothed spurge
	Euphorbia marginata	snow on the mountain
	Euphorbia spathulata	warty spurge
	Tragia betonicifolia	betonyleaf noseburn
Fabaceae	*Amorpha canescens*	leadplant

Family	Scientific Name	Common Name
	Amorpha fruticosa	desert false indigo
	Astragalus canadensis	Canadian milkvetch
	Astragalus crassicarpus	groundplum milkvetch
Fabaceae	*Baptisia alba*	white wild indigo
	Baptisia australis	blue wild indigo
	Baptisia bracteata	longbract wild indigo
	Cercis canadensis	eastern redbud
	Chamaecrista fasciculata	partridge pea
	Dalea candida	white prairie clover
	Dalea multiflora	roundhead prairie clover
	Dalea purpurea	violet prairie clover
	Desmanthus illinoensis	prairie bundleflower
	Desmodium glutinosum	pointedleaf ticktrefoil
	Desmodium illinoense	Illinois ticktrefoil
	Desmodium sessilifolium	sessileleaf ticktrefoil
	Gleditsia triacanthos	honeylocust
	Glycine max	soybean
	Glycyrrhiza lepidota	American licorice
	Gymnocladus dioicus	Kentucky coffeetree
	Lespedeza capitata	roundhead lespedeza
	Lespedeza violacea	violet lespedeza
	Lotus unifoliolatus	American bird's-foot trefoil
	Medicago lupulina	black medick
	Melilotus officinalis	yellow sweetclover
	Mimosa nuttallii	Nuttall's sensitive-briar
	Pediomelum argophyllum	silverleaf Indian breadroot
	Psoralidium tenuiflorum	slimflower scurfpea
	Robinia pseudoacacia	black locust
	Strophostyles leiosperma	slickseed fuzzybean
Fagaceae	*Quercus macrocarpa*	bur oak
	Quercus muehlenbergii	chinkapin oak
Fumariaceae	*Corydalis micrantha*	smallflower fumewort
Gentianaceae	*Gentiana puberulenta*	downy gentian
Geraniaceae	*Geranium carolinianum*	Carolina geranium
Hippocastanaceae	*Aesculus glabra*	Ohio buckeye
Iridaceae	*Sisyrinchium campestre*	prairie blue-eyed grass
Juglandaceae	*Carya texana*	black hickory
	Juglans nigra	black walnut
Juncaceae	*Juncus dudleyi*	Dudley's rush
	Juncus interior	inland rush
	Juncus torreyi	Torrey's rush
Lamiaceae	*Hedeoma hispida*	rough false pennyroyal
	Lamium amplexicaule	henbit deadnettle
	Lycopus americanus	American water horehound
	Monarda fistulosa	wild bergamot
	Prunella vulgaris	common selfheal
	Salvia azurea	azure blue sage

Family	Scientific Name	Common Name
	Scutellaria parvula	small skullcap
	Teucrium canadense	Canada germander
	Trichostema brachiatum	fluxweed
Lemnaceae	*Lemna minor*	common duckweed
Liliaceae	*Allium spp.*	onion
	Erythronium mesochoreum	midland fawnlily
	Nothoscordum bivalve	crowpoison
	Zigadenus nuttallii	Nuttall's deathcamas
Linaceae	*Linum sulcatum*	grooved flax
Loasaceae	*Mentzelia oligosperma*	chickenthief
Lythraceae	*Ammannia coccinea*	valley redstem
	Lythrum alatum	winged lythrum
Malvaceae	*Abutilon theophrasti*	velvetleaf
	Callirhoe alcaeoides	light poppymallow
	Sida spinosa	prickly fanpetals
Menispermaceae	*Menispermum canadense*	moonseed
Molluginaceae	*Mollugo verticillata*	green carpetweed
Moraceae	*Maclura pomifera*	osage orange
	Morus alba	white mulberry
	Morus rubra	red mulberry
Nyctaginaceae	*Mirabilis albida*	white four o'clock
	Mirabilis nyctaginea	heartleaf four o'clock
Oleaceae	*Fraxinus americana*	white ash
	Fraxinus pennsylvanica	green ash
Onagraceae	*Gaura mollis*	velvetweed
	Ludwigia alternifolia	seedbox
	Ludwigia peploides	floating primrose-willow
	Oenothera biennis	common evening-primrose
	Oenothera laciniata	cutleaf evening primrose
	Oenothera macrocarpa	bigfruit evening-primrose
	Oenothera speciosa	pinkladies
Orchidaceae	*Spiranthes cernua*	nodding lady's tresses
Oxalidaceae	*Oxalis stricta*	common yellow oxalis
	Oxalis violacea	violet woodsorrel
Phytolaccaceae	*Phytolacca americana*	American pokeweed
Plantaginaceae	*Plantago rhodosperma*	redseed plantain
	Plantago rugelii	blackseed plantain
	Plantago virginica	Virginia plantain
Platanaceae	*Platanus occidentalis*	American sycamore
Poaceae	*Alopecurus carolinianus*	Carolina foxtail
	Andropogon gerardii	big bluestem
	Aristida oligantha	prairie threeawn
	Bothriochloa laguroides	silver beardgrass
	Bouteloua curtipendula	sideoats grama
	Bouteloua dactyloides	buffalograss
	Bouteloua gracilis	blue grama
	Bouteloua hirsuta	hairy grama

Family	Scientific Name	Common Name
	Bromus arvensis	field brome
	Bromus inermis	smooth brome
	Chloris verticillata	tumble windmill grass
	Dichanthelium acuminatum	tapered rosette grass
	Dichanthelium oligosanthes	Heller's rosette grass
	Dichanthelium wilcoxianum	fall rosette grass
	Digitaria cognata	fall witchgrass
Poaceae	*Digitaria sanguinalis*	hairy crabgrass
	Echinochloa muricata	rough barnyardgrass
	Elymus canadensis	Canada wildrye
	Elymus virginicus	Virginia wildrye
	Eragrostis spectabilis	purple lovegrass
	Festuca subverticillata	nodding fescue
	Glyceria striata	fowl mannagrass
	Koeleria macrantha	prairie Junegrass
	Leersia oryzoides	rice cutgrass
	Leptochloa panicea	mucronate sprangletop
	Muhlenbergia cuspidata	plains muhly
	Muhlenbergia mexicana	Mexican muhly
	Panicum capillare	witchgrass
	Panicum virgatum	switchgrass
	Paspalum pubiflorum	hairyseed paspalum
	Poa pratensis	Kentucky bluegrass
	Schedonorus phoenix	tall fescue
	Schizachyrium scoparium	little bluestem
	Setaria faberi	Japanese bristlegrass
	Setaria pumila	yellow bristlegrass
	Setaria viridis	green bristlegrass
	Sorghastrum nutans	Indiangrass
	Sorghum halepense	Johnsongrass
	Spartina pectinata	prairie cordgrass
	Sphenopholis obtusata	prairie wedgescale
	Sporobolus compositus	composite dropseed
	Sporobolus heterolepis	prairie dropseed
	Sporobolus neglectus	puffsheath dropseed
	Sporobolus vaginiflorus	poverty dropseed
	Tridens flavus	purpletop tridens
	Tripsacum dactyloides	eastern gamagrass
	Vulpia octoflora	sixweeks fescue
Polygalaceae	*Polygala verticillata*	whorled milkwort
Polygonaceae	*Polygonum amphibium*	water knotweed
	Polygonum persicaria	spotted ladysthumb
	Rumex altissimus	pale dock
	Rumex crispus	curly dock
Portulacaceae	*Portulaca oleracea*	little hogweed
Primulaceae	*Androsace occidentalis*	western rockjasmine
Pteridaceae	*Pellaea glabella*	smooth cliffbrake

Family	Scientific Name	Common Name
Ranunculaceae	*Delphinium carolinianum*	Carolina larkspur
	Myosurus minimus	tiny mousetail
Rhamnaceae	*Ceanothus americanus*	New Jersey tea
	Ceanothus herbaceus	Jersey tea
Rosaceae	*Agrimonia parviflora*	harvestlice
	Geum canadense	white avens
	Prunus americana	American plum
	Rosa arkansana	prairie rose
Rubiaceae	*Galium aparine*	stickywilly
Salicaceae	*Populus deltoides*	eastern cottonwood
	Salix interior	sandbar willow
	Salix nigra	black willow
Santalaceae	*Comandra umbellata*	bastard toadflax
Scrophulariaceae	*Leucospora multifida*	narrowleaf paleseed
	Mimulus ringens	Allegheny monkeyflower
	Veronica anagallis-aquatica	water speedwell
	Veronica arvensis	corn speedwell
	Veronica peregrina	neckweed
Solanaceae	*Physalis heterophylla*	clammy groundcherry
	Physalis longifolia	longleaf groundcherry
	Physalis pumila	dwarf groundcherry
	Physalis virginiana	Virginia groundcherry
	Solanum carolinense	Carolina horsenettle
	Solanum rostratum	buffalobur nightshade
Tiliaceae	*Tilia americana*	American basswood
Ulmaceae	*Celtis occidentalis*	common hackberry
	Ulmus americana	American elm
	Ulmus rubra	slippery elm
Urticaceae	*Boehmeria cylindrica*	smallspike false nettle
	Laportea canadensis	Canadian woodnettle
	Parietaria pensylvanica	Pennsylvania pellitory
	Urtica dioica	stinging nettle
Verbenaceae	*Glandularia bipinnatifida*	Dakota mock vervain
	Verbena hastata	swamp verbena
	Verbena simplex	narrowleaf vervain
	Verbena stricta	hoary verbena
	Verbena urticifolia	white vervain
Violaceae	*Hybanthus verticillatus*	babyslippers
	Viola bicolor	field pansy
	Viola nephrophylla	northern bog violet
	Viola pedatifida	prairie violet
Vitaceae	*Parthenocissus quinquefolia*	Virginia creeper

NPS 031/107299, April 2011

Natural Resource Program Center
1201 Oakridge Drive, Suite 150
Fort Collins, CO 80525

www.nature.nps.gov